Teacher Certification Exam

Math Middle School

Written By:

Arlene Gordon Schlessinger, MS Math

Edited By:
Doug Shaw, PhD. Math

To Order Additional Copies:
Xam, Inc.
99 Central St.
Worcester, MA 01605
Toll Free   1-800-301-4647
Phone: 1-508 363 0633
Email: winwin1111@aol.com
Web   www.xamonline.com
EFax   1-501-325-0185
Fax: 1-508-363-0634

You will find:
- Content Review in prose format
- Bibliography
- Sample Test

D1605472

XAM, INC.
Building Better Teachers

"And, while there's no reason yet to panic, I think it's only prudent that we make preparations to panic."

MANKOFF

Printed in the United States of America

Praxis: Math Middle School
ISBN: 1-58197-015-3

TABLE OF CONTENTS

1.0 THE NUMBER SYSTEM

1.1 THE REAL NUMBER SYSTEM

The real number system includes all rational and irrational numbers.

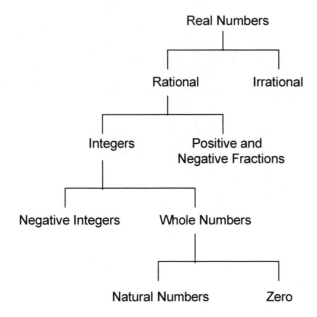

1.2 RATIONAL AND IRRATIONAL NUMBERS

Rational numbers can be expressed as the ratio of two integers, $\frac{a}{b}$ where b ≠ 0, for example $\frac{2}{3}$, $-\frac{4}{5}$, $5 = \frac{5}{1}$.

The rational numbers include integers, fractions and mixed numbers, terminating and repeating decimals. Every rational number can be expressed as a repeating or terminating decimal and can be shown on a number line.

Integers are positive and negative whole numbers and zero.
...-6, -5, -4, -3, -2, -1, 0, 1, 2, 3, 4, 5, 6, ...

Whole numbers are natural numbers and zero.
0, 1, 2, 3, ,4 ,5 ,6 ...

Natural numbers are the counting numbers.
1, 2, 3, 4, 5, 6, ...

Irrational numbers are real numbers that cannot be written as the ratio of two integers. These are infinite non-repeating decimals.
Examples: $\sqrt{5}$ = 2.2360.., pi =∏ = 3.1415927...

"If Heather has two mommies, and each of them has two brothers, and one of those brothers has another man for a 'roommate,' how many uncles does Heather have?"

1.3 COMPLEX NUMBERS

Complex numbers can be written in the form $a + b$i where i represents $\sqrt{-1}$ and a and b are real numbers. a is the real part of the complex number and b is the imaginary part. If $b = 0$, then the number has no imaginary part and it is a real number. If $b \neq 0$, then the number is imaginary.

Complex numbers are found when trying to solve equations with negative square roots.

Example: If $x^2 + 9 = 0$
then $x^2 = -9$
and $x = \sqrt{-9}$ or +3i and -3i

"Mrs. Hammond, I'd know you anywhere from little Billy's portrait of you."

2.0 PROPERTIES OF REAL NUMBERS

2.1 FIELD PROPERTIES

Real numbers exhibit the following addition and multiplication properties, where a, b, and c are real numbers.

Note: Multiplication is implied when there is no symbol between two variables. Thus, $a \times b$ can be written ab. Multiplication can also be indicated by a raised dot ·

Closure
$a + b$ is a real number
Example: Since 2 and 5 are both real numbers, 7 is also a real number.

ab is a real number
Example: Since 3 and 4 are both real numbers, 12 is also a real number.

The sum or product of two real numbers is a real number.

Commutative
$a + b = b + a$
Example: $5 + ^-8 = ^-8 + 5 = ^-3$

$ab = ba$
Example: $^-2 \times 6 = 6 \times ^-2 = ^-12$

The order of the addends or factors does not affect the sum or product.

Associative
$(a + b) + c = a + (b + c)$
Example: $(^-2 + 7) + 5 = ^-2 + (7 + 5)$
$5 + 5 = ^-2 + 12 = 10$

$(ab) c = a (bc)$
Example: $(3 \times ^-7) \times 5 = 3 \times (^-7 \times 5)$
$^-21 \times 5 = 3 \times ^-35 = ^-105$

The grouping of the addends or factors does not affect the sum or product.

Distributive

$a(b + c) = ab + ac$

Example: $6 \times (\,^-4 + 9) = (6 \times \,^-4) + (6 \times 9)$

$\qquad\qquad 6 \times 5 = \,^-24 + 54 = 30$

To multiply a sum by a number, multiply each addend by the number, then add the products.

Additive Identity (Property of Zero)

$a + 0 = a$

Example: $17 + 0 = 17$

The sum of any number and zero is that number.

Multiplicative Identity (Property of One)

$a \cdot 1 = a$

Example: $\,^-34 \times 1 = \,^-34$

The product of any number and one is that number.

Additive Inverse (Property of Opposites)

$a + \,^-a = 0$

Example: $25 + \,^-25 = 0$

The sum of any number and its opposite is zero.

Multiplicative Inverse (Property of Reciprocals)

$a \times \frac{1}{a} = 1$

Example: $5 \times \frac{1}{5} = 1$

The product of any number and its reciprocal is one.

2.2 PROPERTY OF DENSENESS

Between any pair of rational numbers, there is at least one rational number. The set of natural numbers is <u>not</u> dense because between two consecutive natural numbers there may not exist another natural number.

<u>Example:</u>

Between 7.6 and 7.7, there is the rational number 7.65 in the set of real numbers. Between 3 and 4 there exists no other natural number.

2.3 PROPERTIES SATISFIED BY SUBSETS OF REAL NUMBERS

+	Closure	Commutative	Associative	Distributive	Identity	Inverse
Real	yes	yes	yes	yes	yes	yes
Rational	yes	yes	yes	yes	yes	yes
Irrational	yes	yes	yes	yes	no	yes
Integers	yes	yes	yes	yes	yes	yes
Fractions	yes	yes	yes	yes	yes	yes
Whole	yes	yes	yes	yes	yes	no
Natural	yes	yes	yes	yes	no	no

-	Closure	Commutative	Associative	Distributive	Identity	Inverse
Real	yes	no	no	no	yes	yes
Rational	yes	no	no	no	yes	yes
Irrational	no	no	no	no	no	no
Integers	yes	no	no	no	yes	yes
Fractions	yes	no	no	no	yes	yes
Whole	no	no	no	no	yes	no
Natural	no	no	no	no	no	no

×	Closure	Commutative	Associative	Distributive	Identity	Inverse
Real	yes	yes	yes	yes	yes	yes
Rational	yes	yes	yes	yes	yes	yes
Irrational	yes	yes	yes	yes	no	no
Integers	yes	yes	yes	yes	yes	no
Fractions	yes	yes	yes	yes	yes	yes
Whole	yes	yes	yes	yes	yes	no
Natural	yes	yes	yes	yes	yes	no

÷	Closure	Commutative	Associative	Distributive	Identity	Inverse
Real	yes	no	no	no	yes	yes
Rational	yes	no	no	no	yes	yes
Irrational	no	no	no	no	no	no
Integers	no	no	no	no	yes	no
Fractions	yes	no	no	no	yes	yes
Whole	no	no	no	no	yes	no
Natural	no	no	no	no	yes	no

3.0 NUMBER OPERATIONS

3.1 DESCRIPTIONS, DIAGRAMS AND MODELS

Mathematical operations include addition, subtraction, multiplication and division.

Addition can be indicated by the expressions: sum, greater than, and, more than, increased by, added to.

Subtraction can be expressed by: difference, fewer than, minus, less than, decreased by.

Multiplication is shown by: product, times, multiplied by, twice.

Division is used for: quotient, divided by, ratio.

Examples:

7 added to a number	$n + 7$
a number decreased by 8	$n - 8$
12 times a number divided by 7	$12n \div 7$
28 less than a number	$n - 28$
the ratio of a number to 55	$\dfrac{n}{55}$
4 times the sum of a number and 21	$4(n + 21)$

3.2 ORDER OF OPERATIONS

The order of operations has been deveoped to insure uniformity in simplifying expressions. These rules are commonly remembered by the mnemonic
Please Excuse My Dear Aunt Sally.
The letters stand for
Parentheses
Exponents
Multiplication and Division
(in order from left to right)
Addition and Subtraction
(in order from left to right)

Example 1:
$$3 + 4 \cdot 5$$
First multiply, then add. $3 + 20 = 23$

Example 2:
$$7 + 4(2 + 5^2)$$
Work within parentheses first. Raise to power then add.
$$7 + 4(2+25) = 7 + 4(27)$$
First multiply, then add. $7 + 108 = 115$

Example 3:
$$\frac{44 - 2(3^2 + 1)}{16 - 8 \div 2}$$
Work above the bar. $44 - 2(9 + 1) = 44 - 2(10) = 44 - 20 = 24$
Work below the bar. $16 - 4 = 12$
Then divide. $24 \div 12 = 2$

3.3 INVERSE OPERATIONS

Inverse operations are operations that "undo" each other. Addition and subtraction are inverse operations since $3 + 8 = 11$ and $11 - 8 = 3$. Similarly, multiplication and division are inverse operations since $2 \times 7 = 14$ and $14 \div 2 = 7$.

Inverse operations are used to solve equations.

Example 1: $x + 12 = 17$ Subtract 12 from each side of the equation

$\qquad\qquad \dfrac{-12 \quad -12}{x \quad = \quad 5}$ since the inverse of addition is subtraction.

Example 2: $4x = {}^-20$ Divide both sides of the equation by 4

$\qquad\qquad \dfrac{4x}{4} = \dfrac{-20}{4}$ since the inverse of multiplication is division.

$\qquad\qquad x = {}^-5$

3.4 ESTIMATION AND APPROXIMATION

Estimation and approximation may be used to check the reasonableness of answers.

<u>Example</u>: Estimate the answer.
$$\frac{58 \times 810}{1989}$$

810 becomes 800 and 1989 is 2000.
$$\frac{60 \times 800}{2000} = 24$$

Word problems: An estimate may sometimes be all that is needed to solve a problem.

<u>Example</u>: Janet has $50. Shoes are $9.95, a blouse is $19.95 and shorts are $14.59. Does she have enough money?

Round $9.95 to $10, $19.95 to $20 and $14.50 to $15. Adding, $10 + 20 + 15 = 45$ so Janet has enough money.

4.0 NUMBER THEORY

4.1 GREATEST COMMON FACTOR (GCF) AND
LEAST COMMON MULTIPLE (LCM)

When two or more numbers are multiplied to give a certain product, each of these numbers is called a **factor** of the product. Factors can most easily be derived in pairs.

Example: The factors of 24 are:
$$1 \times 24 = 24$$
$$2 \times 12 = 24$$
$$3 \times 8 = 24$$
$$4 \times 6 = 24$$
The factors of 24 are: 1, 2, 3, 4, 6, 8, 12, 24.

The **Greatest Common Factor** (GCF) of two numbers is the largest factor that they share.

Example 1: Find the GCF of 20 and 30
    20:   1, 2, 4, 5, **10**, 20
    30:   1, 2, 3, 5, 6, **10**, 15, 30
The greatest common factor of 20 and 30 is 10

Example 2: Find the GCF of 12 and 18
    12:   1, 2, 3, 4, **6**, 12
    18;   1, 2, 3, **6**, 9, 18
The greatest common factor of 12 and 18 is 6.

A **multiple** is a number that is the *product* of the given number and another *factor*. Multiples are commonly listed in consecutive order.

Example: The multiples of 5 would be calculated by multiplying
    $5 \times 1, 5 \times 2, 5 \times 3, 5 \times 4, 5 \times 5, 5 \times 6$, and so on.
    Thus, the multiples of 5 are: 5, 10, 15, 20, 25, 30,...

The **Least Common Multiple** (LCM) of two numbers is the smallest multiple they share.

Example1: Find the LCM of 4 and 6.
  Multiples of 4 are: 4, 8, **12,** 16, 20, 24, ...
  Multiples of 6 are: 6, **12,** 18, 24, 30, 36, ...
  Although 12 and 24 are *both* common multiples of 4 and 6,
  the LCM is 12 because it is less than 24.

Example 2: Find the LCM of 8 and 10.
  8: 8, 16, 24, 32, 40, 48, ...
  10: 10, 20, 30, 40, ...
  40 is the least common multiple of 8 and 10.

4.2 DIVISIBILITY TESTS (DIVISORS 2, 3, 4, 5, 6, 8, 9, 10)

A number, x, is divisible by another number, y, when the second number, y, is a factor of the first number, x. Thus x can be divided by y with no remainder. This can be determined, without actually dividing, by some simple rules.

A number is divisible by **2** when **it <u>ends</u> in 0, 2, 4, 6,** or **8.**

Example: 31<u>2</u>, 777<u>4</u>

A number is divisible by **5** when **it <u>ends</u> in 0** or **5.**

Example: 93<u>5</u>, 87<u>0</u>

A number is divisible by **10** when **it <u>ends</u> in 0.**

Example: 973<u>0</u>, 520<u>0</u>

A number is divisible by **3** when **the <u>sum</u> of its digits is divisible by 3.**

Example: 744, 8511

A number is divisible by **9** when **the <u>sum</u> of its digits is divisible by 9.**

Example: 837, 8928

Additional explanation of examples: 744: $7 + 4 + 4 = 15$ which is divisible by 3, therefore 744 is divisible by 3. Similarly, 837: $8 + 3 + 7 = 18$ which is divisible by 9, therefore 837 is divisible by 9 (and also by 3).

A number is divisible by **4** when **its last <u>two</u> digits are divisible by 4.**

Example: 3<u>28</u>, 13<u>64</u>

A number is divisible by **8** when **its last <u>three</u> digits are divisible by 8.**

Example: 9<u>248</u>, 13<u>720</u>

Additional explanation of examples: 328: 28 divided by 4 is 7, therefore 328 is divisible by 4. Similarly, 9248: 248 divided by 8 is 31, therefore 9248 is divisible by 8. (Interesting fact: all election years are divisible by 4, thus their last two digits are divisible by 4.)

A number is divisible by **6** when **it <u>ends</u> in 0, 2, 4, 6,** or **8** *and* **the <u>sum</u> of its digits is divisible by 3**. In other words, when **it is divisible by both 2 and 3**

<u>Example</u>: 516, 3852

Additional explanation of example: 516 is divisible by 2 since its last digit is 6 and the sum of its digits is $5 + 1 + 6 = 12$ which is divisible by 3. Therefore 516 is divisible by 6.

<u>Example 1</u>: 7314 is divisible by:
  2 because it ends in 4
  3 because $7 + 3 + 4 + 1 = 15$
  6 because it is divisible by both 2 and 3

<u>Example 2</u>: 6624 is divisible by
  2 because is ends in 4
  3 and 9 because $6 + 6 + 2 + 4 = 18$
  4 because 24 is divisible by 4
  6 because it is divisible by both 2 and 3

4.3 PRIME AND COMPOSITE NUMBERS

A **prime** number has exactly <u>two</u> factors, itself and one. A **composite** number has more than two factors. 0 and 1 are *neither* prime nor composite.

Example: **Prime:** The only factors of 7 are 1 and 7, therefore 7 is prime.
The number two is the only even prime.

Composite: The factors of 18 are: 1, 2, 3, 6, 9, and 18 .
Therefore the number 18 has more than two factors and is considered composite.

4.4 PRIME FACTORIZATION

Any number can be written as the product of its prime factors. Every composite number can always be expressed as the product of prime factors.

A **factor tree** can be used to show the prime factorization of a number. A factor tree can be started with any two factors, but the prime factorization will always be the same.

Example:

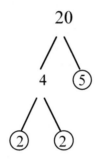

Thus $20 = 2 \times 2 \times 5 = 2^2 \times 5$

5.0 NUMERATION AND EXPONENTS

5.1 EXPONENTS AND DECIMALS

The **exponent form** is a shortcut method to write repeated multiplication. The **base** is the factor. The **exponent** tells how many times that number is multiplied by itself.

Example: 3^4 is $3 \times 3 \times 3 \times 3 = 81$
  where 3 is the base and 4 is the exponent.

x^2 *is read* "x squared"
y^3 *is read* "y cubed"

a^1 = a for all values of a; thus $17^1 = 17$
b^0 = 1 for all values of b; thus $24^0 = 1$

When 10 is raised to any power, the exponent tells the numbers of zeroes in the product.

Example: $10^7 = 10,000,000$

5.2 SCIENTIFIC NOTATION

Scientific notation is a more convenient method for writing very large and very small numbers. It employs two factors. The **first factor** is a **number between 1 and 10**. The **second factor** is a **power of 10**.

Example 1: Write 372,000 in scientific notation
      Move the decimal point to form a number between 1 and 10; thus 3.72.
      Since the decimal point was moved 5 places, the power of 10 is 10^5.
      The exponent is positive since the decimal point was moved to the left.
$$372,000 = 3.72 \times 10^5$$

Example 2: Write 0.0000072 in scientific notation.
      Move the decimal point 6 places to the right.
$$0.0000072 = 7.2 \times 10^{-6}$$

Example 3: Write 2.19×10^8 in standard form.
      Since the exponent is positive, move the decimal point 8 places to the right,
      and add additional zeroes as needed.
$$2.19 \times 10^8 = 219,000,000$$

Example 4: Write 8.04×10^{-4} in standard form.
      Move the decimal point 4 places to the left, writing additional zeroes as needed.
$$8.04 \times 10^{-4} = 0.000804$$

** Note: The first factor **must** be between 1 and 10.

6.0 RATIOS, PROPORTIONS, AND PERCENTS

6.1 PROPORTIONS

A **ratio** is a comparison of two numbers. A **proportion** is a statement that two ratios are equivalent. Proportions can be solved by using cross-products.

$$\text{Example:} \quad \frac{n}{12} = \frac{7}{14}$$

$n \times 14 = 7 \times 12$ Multiply to find the cross-product.

$14\,n = 84$

$$\frac{14n}{14} = \frac{84}{14}$$ Divide both sides of the equation by 14.

$n = 6$

6.2 USING PROPORTIONS TO SOLVE WORD PROBLEMS

Proportions can be used to solve word problems whenever relationships are compared. Some situations include scale drawings and maps, similar polygons, speed, time and distance, cost, and comparison shopping.

<u>Example 1</u>: Which is the better buy, 6 items for $1.29 or 8 items for $1.69?

Find the unit price.

$$\frac{6}{1.29} = \frac{1}{x} \qquad\qquad \frac{8}{1.69} = \frac{1}{x}$$
$$6x = 1.29 \qquad\qquad 8x = 1.69$$
$$x = 0.215 \qquad\qquad x = 0.21125$$

Thus, 8 items for $1.69 is the better buy.

<u>Example 2</u>: A car travels 125 miles in 2.5 hours.. How far will it go in 6 hours?

Write a proportion comparing the distance and time.

$$\frac{miles}{hours} \qquad \frac{125}{2.5} = \frac{x}{6}$$
$$2.5x = 750$$
$$x = 300$$

Thus, the car can travel 300 miles in 6 hours.

<u>Example 3</u>: The scale on a map is $\frac{3}{4}$ inch $= 6$ miles. What is the actual distance between   two cities if they are $1\frac{1}{2}$ inches apart on the map?

Write a proportion comparing the scale to the actual distance.

$$\begin{array}{cc} \text{scale} & \text{actual} \end{array}$$
$$\frac{\frac{3}{4}}{1\frac{1}{2}} = \frac{6}{x}$$
$$\tfrac{3}{4}x = 1\tfrac{1}{2} \times 6$$
$$\tfrac{3}{4}x = 9$$
$$x = 12$$

Thus, the actual distance between the cities is 12 miles.

6.3 EQUIVALENT FRACTIONS, DECIMALS, AND PERCENTS

Percent means parts of one hundred. Fractions, decimals and percents can be interchanged.

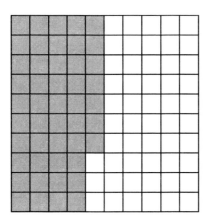

The shaded region represents 47 out of 100 or 0.47 or $\frac{47}{100}$ or 47%.

$100\% = 1$

If a fraction can easily be converted to an equivalent **fraction** whose denominator is a power of 10 (for example, 10, 100, 1000), then it can easily be expressed as a **decimal** or **%.**

Examples: $\frac{1}{10} = 0.10 = 10\%$

$\frac{2}{5} = \frac{4}{10} = 0.40 = 40\%$

$\frac{1}{4} = \frac{25}{100} = 0.25 = 25\%$

Alternately, the **fraction** can be converted to a **decimal** and then a **percent** by dividing the numerator by the denominator, adding a decimal point and zeroes.

Example: $\frac{3}{8} = 8\overline{)3.000}^{\,0.375} = 37.5\%$

A **decimal** can be converted to a **percent** by multiplying by 100, or merely moving the decimal point two places to the right. A **percent** can be converted to a **decimal** by dividing by 100, or moving the decimal point two places to the left.

Examples: $0.375 = 37.5\%$
$0.7 = 70\%$
$0.04 = 4\%$
$3.15 = 315\%$

$84\% = 0.84$
$3\% = 0.03$
$60\% = 0.6$
$110\% = 1.1$
$\frac{1}{2}\% = 0.5\% = 0.005$

A **percent** can be converted to a **fraction** by placing it over 100 and reducing to simplest terms.

Examples: $32\% = \frac{32}{100} = \frac{8}{25}$
$6\% = \frac{6}{100} = \frac{3}{50}$
$111\% = \frac{111}{100} = 1\frac{11}{100}$

6.4 WORD PROBLEMS WITH PERCENTS

Word problems involving percents can be solved by writing the problem as an equation, then solving the equation. Keep in mind that **"of"** means **"multiplication"** and **"is"** means **"equals."**

Example 1: The Ski Club has 85 members. 80% of the members are able to attend the meeting. How many members attend the meeting?

Restate the problem. What is 80% of 85?
Write an equation. $n = 0.8 \times 85$
Solve. $n = 68$

Sixty-eight members attend the meeting.

Example 2: There are 64 dogs in the kennel. 48 are collies. What percent are collies?

Restate the problem. 48 is what percent of 64?
Write an equation. $48 = n \times 64$
Solve. $\frac{48}{64} = n$
                      $n = \frac{3}{4} = 75\%$

75% of the dogs are collies.

Example 3: The auditorium was filled to 90% capacity. There were 558 seats occupied. What is the capacity of the auditorium?

Restate the problem. 90% of what number is 558?
Write an equation. $0.9n = 558$
Solve. $n = \frac{558}{.9}$
                      $n = 620$

The capacity of the auditorium is 620 people.

Example 4: Shoes cost $42.00. Sales tax is 6%. What is the total cost of the shoes?

Restate the problem. What is 6% of 42?
Write an equation. $n = 0.06 \times 42$
Solve. $n = 2.50$ 2.52

Add the sales tax to the cost. $42.00 + $2.50 = $44.50

The total cost of the shoes, including sales tax, is $44.50.

5 2/a

COMMON EQUIVALENTS

$\frac{1}{2} = 0.5 = 50\%$

$\frac{1}{3} = 0.33\frac{1}{3} = 33\frac{1}{3}\%$

$\frac{1}{4} = 0.25 = 25\%$

$\frac{1}{5} = 0.2 = 20\%$

$\frac{1}{6} = 0.16\frac{2}{3} = 16\frac{2}{3}\%$

$\frac{1}{8} = 0.12\frac{1}{2} = 12\frac{1}{2}\%$

$\frac{1}{10} = 0.1 = 10\%$

$\frac{2}{3} = 0.66\frac{2}{3} = 66\frac{2}{3}\%$

$\frac{5}{6} = 0.83\frac{1}{3} = 83\frac{1}{3}\%$

$\frac{3}{8} = 0.37\frac{1}{2} = 37\frac{1}{2}\%$

$\frac{5}{8} = 0.62\frac{1}{2} = 62\frac{1}{2}\%$

$\frac{7}{8} = 0.87\frac{1}{2} = 87\frac{1}{2}\%$

$1 = 1.0 = 100\%$

7.0 PROBABILITY

7.1 DEPENDENT and INDEPENDENT EVENTS

Probability measures the chances of an event occurring. The probability of an event that *must* occur, a certain event, is **one**. When no outcome is favorable, the probability of an impossible event is **zero**.

$$P \text{ (event)} = \frac{number\ of\ favorable\ outcomes}{number\ of\ possible\ outcomes}$$

Example: Given one die with faces numbered 1 - 6, the probability of tossing an even number on one throw of the die is $\frac{3}{6}$ or $\frac{1}{2}$ since there are 3 favorable outcomes (even faces) and a total of 6 possible outcomes (faces).

If A and B are **independent** events then the probability both A and B will occur is the product of their individual probabilities.

Example 1: Given two dice, the probability of tossing a 3 on each of them simultaneously is the probability of a 3 on the first die, or $\frac{1}{6}$, times the probability of tossing a 3 on the second die, also $\frac{1}{6}$.

$$\frac{1}{6} \times \frac{1}{6} = \frac{1}{36}$$

Example 2: Given a jar containing 10 marbles, 3 red, 5 black, and 2 white. What is the probability of drawing a red marble and then a white marble if the marble is returned to the jar after choosing?

$$\frac{3}{10} \times \frac{2}{10} = \frac{6}{100} = \frac{3}{50}$$

When the outcome of the first event affects the outcome of the second event, the events are **dependent**. Any two events that are not independent are dependent. This is also known as conditional probability.

Probability of (A and B) = P(A) × P(B given A)

Example: Two cards are drawn from a deck of 52 cards, without replacement; that is, the first card is not returned to the deck before the second card is drawn. What is the probability of drawing a diamond?

A = drawing a diamond first
B = drawing a diamond second
$P(A) = \frac{13}{52} = \frac{1}{4}$ $P(B) = \frac{12}{51} = \frac{4}{17}$
$P(A + B) = \frac{1}{4} \times \frac{4}{17} = \frac{1}{17}$

"Are we there yet?"

7.2 ODDS

The **odds** of an event occurring is the ratio of the number of favorable outcomes to the number of unfavorable outcomes.

Example: Given one die with faces numbered 1 - 6,
        the odds of tossing an even number is

$$\frac{number\ of\ favorable\ outcomes}{number\ of\ unfavorable\ outcomes} = \frac{3}{3} = \frac{1}{1} \text{or 1 to 1 or even chances.}$$

8.0 STATISTICS

8.1 MEAN, MEDIAN, MODE, AND RANGE.

The arithmetic **mean** (or average) of a set of numbers is the *sum* of the numbers given, *divided* by the number of items being averaged.

Example: Find the mean. Round to the nearest tenth.
24.6, 57.3, 44.1, 39.8, 64.5
The sum is $230.3 \div 5 = 46.06$, rounded to 46.1

The **median** of a set is the middle number. To calculate the median, the terms must be arranged in order. If there are an even number of terms, the median is the mean of the two middle terms.

Example 1: Find the median.
12, 14, 27, 3, 13, 7, 17, 12, 22, 6, 16
Rearrange the terms.
3, 6, 7, 12, 12, **13**, 14, 16, 17, 22, 27
Since there are 11 numbers, the middle would be the sixth number or 13.

Example 2: Find the median.
43, 16, 7, 4, 19, 28
Rearrange the terms.
4, 7, **16, 19**, 28, 43
Since there are 6 numbers, the median is the average of 16 and 19 or 17.5

The **mode** of a set of numbers is the number that occurs with the greatest frequency. A set can have no mode if each term appears exactly one time. Similarly, there can also be more than one mode.

Example 1: Find the mode.
26, 15, 37, **26**, 35, **26**, 15
15 appears twice, but 26 appears 3 times, therefore the mode is 26.

Example 2: Find the mode.
38, **14**, **6**, **14**, 9, 36, **6**, 47
Since both 6 and 14 appear twice, there are two modes, 6 and 14.

The **range** of a set of data is the difference between the largest and smallest values.

<u>Example</u>: Find the range.

6, 17, 35, 24, 8, 3, 17, 24, 31

Since the smallest number is 3 and the largest is 35, the range is the difference between 35 - 3 or 32.

8.2 MEASURE OF CENTRAL TENDENCY

The **measures of central tendency** are the mean, median and mode. Different situations can best be described by each of these.

Example 1: Is the mean, median, or mode the best measure of central tendency for the set 135, 135, 137, 190?

The mean is 149.25, the median is 136 and the mode is 135, therefore, the median or mode would be a better measure than the mean since they are both closer to most of the scores.

Example 2: The yearly salaries of the employees of Company A are $11,000, $12,000, $12,000, $15,000, $20,000, and $25,000. Which measure of central tendency would you use if you were a manager? if you were an employee trying to get a raise?

The mean is $15,833
The median is $13,500
The mode is $12,000
The manager would probably use the mean since it is the largest amount. The employee would most likely use the mode since is the smallest.

8.3 BAR, LINE, PICTO-, AND CIRCLE GRAPHS

	Test 1	Test 2	Test 3	Test 4	Test 5
Evans, Tim	75	66	80	85	97
Miller, Julie	94	93	88	97	98
Thomas, Randy	81	86	88	87	90

Bar graphs are used to compare various quantities.

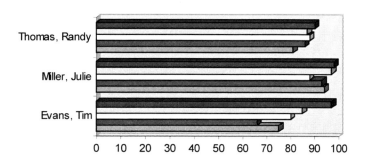

Line graphs are used to show trends, often over a period of time.

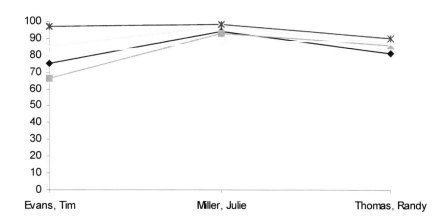

A **pictograph** shows comparison of quantities using symbols. Each symbol represents a number of items.

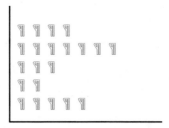

Circle graphs show the relationship of various parts to each other and the whole. Percents are used to create circle graphs.

Julie spends 8 hours each day in school, 2 hours doing homework, 1 hour eating dinner, 2 hours watching television, 10 hours sleeping and the rest of the time doing other things.

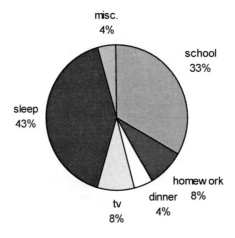

8.4 APPLY BASIC CONCEPTS

Basic statistical concepts can be applied without computations. For example, inferences can be drawn from a graph or statistical data. A bar graph could display which grade level collected the most money. Student test scores would enable the teacher to determine which units need to be remediated.

9. APPROPRIATE MEASUREMENT

"When you can measure what you are speaking about and express it in numbers, you know something about it; but when you cannot measure it, when you cannot express it in numbers, your knowledge is of a meagre and unsatisfactory kind." Lord Kelvin

Non-standard units are sometimes used when standard instruments might not be available. For example, students might measure the length of a room by their arm-spans. An inch originated as the length of three barley grains placed end to end. Seeds or stones might be used for measuring weight. In fact, our current "carat," used for measuring precious gems, was derived from carob seeds. In ancient times, baskets, jars and bowls were used to measure capacity.

To estimate measurement of familiar objects, it is first necessary to determine the units to be used.

Examples:
Length
1. The coastline of Florida   miles or kilometers
2. The width of a ribbon   inches or millimeters
3. The thickness of a book   inches or centimeters
4. The length of a football field   yards or meters
5. The depth of water in a pool   feet or meters

Weight or mass
1. A bag of sugar   pounds or grams
2. A school bus   tons or kilograms
3. A dime   ounces or grams

Capacity
1. Paint to paint a bedroom   gallons or liters
2. Glass of milk   cups or liters
3. Bottle of soda   quarts or liters
4. Medicine for child   ounces or milliliters

10.   MEASUREMENT

10.1 ESTIMATING MEASUREMENT

The sizes of familiar objects can be estimated to obtain a general idea or comparison.

Examples: Estimate the measurements of the following objects.

length of a dollar bill	6 in.
weight of a baseball	1 pound
distance from New York to Florida	1100 km
amount of water to fill a medicine dropper	1 milliliter
length of a desk	2 meters
temperature of water in swimming pool	80°

10.2   MEASURING TO THE NEAREST UNIT

Depending on the degree of accuracy needed, an object may be measured to different units. For example, a pencil may be 6 inches to the nearest inch, or $6\frac{3}{8}$ inches to the nearest eighth of an inch. Similarly, it might be 15 cm to the nearest cm or 154 mm to the nearest mm.

10.3 CONVERTING UNITS

CUSTOMARY SYSTEM

The units of **length** in the customary system are inches, feet, yards and miles.

> 12 inches (in.) = 1 foot (ft.)
> 36 in. = 1 yard (yd.)
> 3 ft. = 1 yd.
> 5280 ft. = 1 mile (mi.)
> 1760 yd. = 1 mi.

To change from a **larger unit to a smaller unit, multiply**.
To change from a **smaller unit to a larger unit, divide**.

Example 1:
        4 mi. = _____ yd.
        Since 1760 yd. = 1 mile, multiply $4 \times 1760 = 7040$ yd.

Example 2:
        21 in. = _____ ft.
        $21 \div 12 = 1\frac{3}{4}$ ft.

The units of **weight** are ounces, pounds and tons.

> 16 ounces (oz.) = 1 pound (lb.)
> 2,000 lb. = 1 ton (T.)

Example: $2\frac{3}{4}$ T. = _____ lb.
        $2\frac{3}{4} \times 2,000 = 5,500$ lb.

The units of **capacity** are fluid ounces, cups, pints, quarts, and gallons.

> 8 fluid ounces (fl. oz.) = 1 cup (c.)
> 2 c. = 1 pint (pt.)
> 4 c. = 1 quart (qt.)
> 2 pt. = 1 qt.
> 4 qt. = 1 gallon (gal.)

Example1: 3 gal. = _____ qt.
$3 \times 4 = 12$ qt.

Example 2: $1\frac{1}{4}$ cups = _____ oz.
$1\frac{1}{4} \times 8 = 10$ oz.

Example 3: 7 c. = _____ pt.
$7 \div 2 = 3\frac{1}{2}$ pt.

Square units can be derived with knowledge of basic units of length by squaring the equivalent measurements.

> 1 square foot (sq. ft.) = 144 sq. in.
> 1 sq. yd. = 9 sq. ft.
> 1 sq. yd. = 1296 sq. in.

Example: 14 sq. yd. = _____ sq. ft.
$14 \times 9 = 126$ sq. ft.

METRIC UNITS

The metric system is based on multiples of <u>ten</u>. Conversions are made by simply moving the decimal point to the left or right.

kilo-   1000   thousands
hecto-   100   hundreds
deca-   10   tens
unit
deci-   .1   tenths
centi-   .01   hundredths
milli-   .001   thousandths

The basic unit for **length** is the meter. One meter is approximately one yard.
The basic unit for **weight** or mass is the gram. A paper clip weighs about one gram.
The basic unit for **volume** is the liter. One liter is approximately a quart.

These are the most commonly used units.

1 m = 100 cm	1000 mL= 1 L	1000 mg = 1 g
1 m = 1000 mm	1 kL = 1000 L	1 kg = 1000 g
1 cm = 10 mm		
1000 m = 1 km		

The prefixes are commonly listed from left to right for ease in conversion.

K   H   D   U   D   C   M

Example 1:   63 km = _____ m
Since there are 3 steps from <u>K</u>ilo to <u>U</u>nit, move the decimal point 3 places to the right.
        63 km = 63,000 m

Example 2:   14 mL = _____ L
Since there are 3 steps from <u>M</u>illi to <u>U</u>nit, move the decimal point 3 places to the left.
        14 mL = 0.014 L

Example 3:   56.4 cm = _____ mm
        56.4 cm = 564 mm

Example 4:   9.1 m = _____ km
        9.1 m = 0.0091 km

Example 5:   75 kg = _____ mg
        75 kg = 75,000,000 mg

10.4   ACCURACY, PRECISION and GREATEST POSSIBLE ERROR

The **precision** of a measurement is related to the unit that is used. The smaller the unit, the more precise the measurement will be. Thus, 42 mm is more accurate than 4 cm.

The amount of precision or **greatest possible error (GPE)** is equal to one-half of the smallest unit of measurement that is used. For example, if the smallest unit was mm, then the greatest possible error would be $\pm\frac{1}{2}$ mm.

Similarly, if the smallest unit was $\frac{1}{2}$ inch, then the greatest possible error would be $\frac{1}{2} \times \frac{1}{2} = \pm\frac{1}{4}$ inch.

The greatest possible error can be used to find the range of a measurement by adding and subtracting the greatest possible error from that measurement.

<u>Example 1</u>: If the measurement is 93 miles, the GPE is $\pm\frac{1}{2}$ mile and the range of measurement is between $92\frac{1}{2}$ miles and $93\frac{1}{2}$ miles.

<u>Example 2</u>: If the measurement is 18.3 cm, the GPE is ±0.05 cm and the range is 18.25 - 18.35 cm.

11. PERIMETER AND AREA

11.1 PERIMETER AND AREA OF POLYGONS

The **perimeter** of any polygon is the sum of the lengths of the sides.

P = sum of sides

Since the opposite sides of a rectangle are congruent, the perimeter of a rectangle equals twice the sum of the length and width or

$P_{rect} = 2l + 2w$ or $2(l + w)$

Similarly, since all the sides of a square have the same measure, the perimeter of a square equals four times the length of one side or

$P_{square} = 4s$

The **area** of a polygon is the number of square units covered by the figure.

$A_{rect} = l \times w$
$A_{square} = s^2$

Example 1: Find the perimeter and the area of this rectangle.

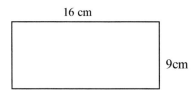

16 cm

9cm

$P_{rect} = 2l + 2w$ $A_{rect} = l \times w$
     $= 2(16) + 2(9)$ $= 16(9)$
     $= 32 + 18 = 50$ cm $= 144$ cm^2

Example 2: Find the perimeter and area of this square.

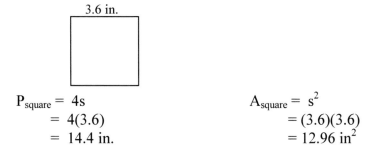

3.6 in.

$P_{square} = 4s$ $A_{square} = s^2$
       $= 4(3.6)$ $= (3.6)(3.6)$
       $= 14.4$ in. $= 12.96$ in^2

11.2   CIRCUMFERENCE AND AREA OF CIRCLES

The distance around a circle is the **circumference**. The ratio of the circumference to the radius is represented by the Greek letter pi. $\Pi \sim 3.14 \sim \dfrac{22}{7}$.

The circumference of a circle is found by the formula $C = 2\Pi r$ or $C = \Pi d$ where r is the radius of the circle and d is the diameter.

The **area** of a circle is found by the formula $A = \Pi r^2$.

Example: Find the circumference and area of a circle whose radius is 7 meters.

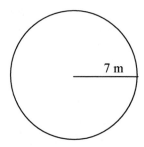

7 m

$C = 2\Pi r$

$= 2(3.14)(7)$

$= 43.96 \text{ m}$

$A = \Pi r^2$

$= 3.14(7)(7)$

$= 153.86 \text{ m}^2$

11.3 AREAS OF PARALLELOGRAMS, TRIANGLES and TRAPEZOIDS

In the following formulas, b = the base
and h = the height of an altitude drawn to the base.

$A_{parallelogram} = bh$

$A_{triangle} = \frac{1}{2}bh$

$A_{trapezoid} = \frac{1}{2}h(b_1 + b_2)$

<u>Example 1:</u> Find the area of a parallelogram whose base is 6.5 cm and the height of the altitude to that base is 3.7 cm.

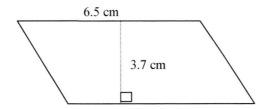

6.5 cm

3.7 cm

$A_{parallelogram} = bh$

$= (3.7)(6.5)$
$= 24.05 \text{ cm}^2$

<u>Example 2:</u> Find the area of this triangle.

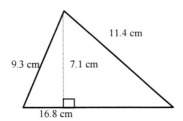

11.4 cm

9.3 cm   7.1 cm

16.8 cm

$A_{triangle} = \frac{1}{2}bh$
$= 0.5\,(16.8)\,(7.1)$
$= 59.64 \text{ cm}^2$

Note that the altitude is drawn to the base measuring 16.8 cm. The lengths of the other two sides is unnecessary information.

<u>Example 3:</u> Find the area of a right triangle whose sides measure 10 inches, 24 inches and 26 inches.

Since the hypotenuse of a right triangle must be the longest side, then the two perpendicular sides must measure 10 and 24 inches.

$$A_{triangle} = \tfrac{1}{2}bh$$
$$= \tfrac{1}{2}(10)(24)$$
$$= 120 \text{ sq. in.}$$

<u>Example 4:</u> Find the area of this trapezoid.

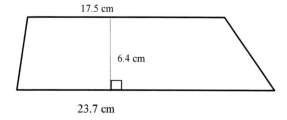

17.5 cm

6.4 cm

23.7 cm

The area of a trapezoid equals one-half the sum of the bases times the altitude.

$$A_{trapezoid} = \tfrac{1}{2}h(b_1 + b_2)$$
$$= 0.5(6.4)(17.5 + 23.7)$$
$$= 131.84 \text{ cm}^2$$

11.4 and 11.5   IRREGULAR POLYGONS

The areas of irregular shaped figures can be calculated by dividing them into rectangles, triangles, parallelograms, and so on.

<u>Example:</u>   Find the area.

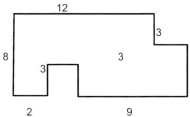

Divide the figure into rectangles.

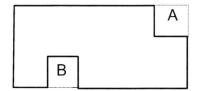

The area of the large rectangle is (12 + 3) × 8 = 120

The area of rectangle A (which is also a square) is 3 × 3 = 9

The missing piece of rectangle B can be found by determining the total length of the rectangle which is 12 + 3 = 15, then subtracting the known lengths of 2 + 9 = 11. Thus the missing piece is 15 - 11 = 4.

The area of rectangle B = 4 × 3 = 12

The total area of the figure is the large rectangle minus the areas of the two small rectangles.

150 - 9 - 12 = 99 square units

11.6 SIMILAR POLYGONS

The perimeters of similar polygons are proportional.

The areas of similar polygons are in that ratio, squared.

<u>Example 1</u>: If the ratio of the sides of similar polygons is $\dfrac{2}{3}$

then the ratio of their perimeters is $\dfrac{2}{3}$.

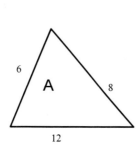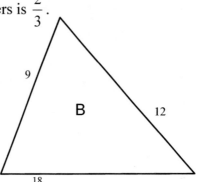

The perimeter of triangle A is $6 + 8 + 12 = 26$
The perimeter of triangle B is $9 + 12 + 18 = 39$

$$\frac{26}{39} = \frac{2}{3}$$

<u>Example 2</u>: If the ratio of the sides of similar polygons is $\dfrac{2}{3}$

then the ratio of their areas is $\dfrac{4}{9}$

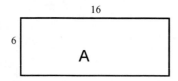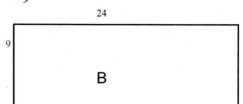

The area of rectangle A is $6 \times 16 = 96$
The area of rectangle B is $9 \times 24 = 216$

$$\frac{96 \div 24}{216 \div 24} = \frac{4}{9}$$

12. SURFACE AREAS AND VOLUME

12.1   RIGHT PRISMS AND REGULAR PYRAMIDS

The **lateral** area is the area of the faces excluding the base.

The **surface area** is the total area of all the faces, including the base.

The **volume** is the number of cubic units in a solid. This is the amount of space a figure holds.

<u>Right prism</u>

$V = Bh$ (where B = area of the base of the prism and h = the height of the prism)

<u>Rectangular right prism</u>

$S = 2(lw + hw + lh)$ (where l = length, w = width and h = height)
$V = lwh$

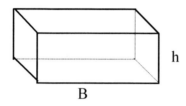

<u>Example</u>: Find the height of a box whose volume is 120 cubic meters and the area of the base is 30 square meters.

$$V = Bh$$
$$120 = 30h$$
$$h = 4 \text{ meters}$$

<u>Regular pyramid</u>

$V = \frac{1}{3}Bh$

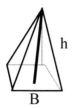

12.2   RIGHT CIRCULAR CYLINDERS and CONES

Right circular cylinder

$S = 2\Pi r(r + h)$ (where r is the radius of the base)
$V = \Pi r^2 h$

Right circular cone

$V = \frac{1}{3} Bh$

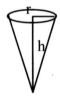

12.3   SPHERES

Sphere

$S = 4\Pi r^2$
$V = \frac{4}{3}\Pi r^3$

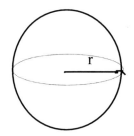

13. AXIOMS OF EQUALITY

The **reflexive**, **symmetric**, and **transitive** properties are known as the **Axioms of Equality**. For all real numbers a, b, and c:

Reflexive $a = a$

Symmetric   If $a = b$ then $b = a$

Transitive   If $a = b$ and $b = c$, the $a = c$

Example: Transitive Property
        If $x = 2 + 3$ and $2 + 3 = 5$, then $x = 5$

14. RATIONAL EXPRESSIONS

SIMPLIFYING RATIONAL EXPRESSIONS

A **rational expression** or a rational algebraic expression is the quotient of two polynomials. The divisor can <u>never</u> be zero.

A rational expression is in **simplest form** when the numerator and denominator have no common factor except for 1 or ⁻1. To simplify a rational expression, factor the numerator and denominator completely, then divide by their common factors.

Example: Simplify $\dfrac{4x^3 - 4x^2 + x}{4x^3 - x}$

$$\dfrac{x(4x^2 - 4x + 1)}{x(4x^2 - 1)}$$

$\dfrac{x(2x-1)(2x-1)}{x(2x-1)(2x+1)}$ Divide the numerator and denominator
                                   by $x(2x-1)$

$$\dfrac{2x-1}{2x+1}$$

ADDING AND SUBTRACTING RATIONAL EXPRESSIONS

Rational expressions having the same denominator can be **added** and **subtracted** using the same rules as rational numbers. If the denominators differ, you must first find a common denominator before adding or subtracting.

Example 1:
$$\frac{6}{4y-2} - \frac{2y+4}{4y-2}$$

$$\frac{-2y+2}{4y-2}$$ Add the numerators.

$$\frac{2(-y+1)}{2(2y-1)} = \frac{1-y}{2y-1}$$ Simplify.

Example 2:
$$\frac{3}{6a^2} - \frac{9}{2a}$$

$$\frac{3}{6a^2} - \frac{9(3a)}{2a(3a)}$$ Find a common denominator.

$$\frac{3}{6a^2} - \frac{27a}{6a^2}$$ Subtract.

$$\frac{3-27a}{6a^2}$$ Simplify.

$$\frac{3(1-9a)}{3(2a^2)} = \frac{1-9a}{2a^2}$$

Example 3: $\dfrac{p+q}{p^2+2pq+q^2} + \dfrac{2p}{p^2-q^2}$

$\dfrac{p+q}{(p+q)(p+q)} + \dfrac{2p}{(p+q)(p-q)}$ Factor to find LCD.

$\dfrac{(p+q)(p-q)}{(p+q)(p+q)(p-q)} + \dfrac{2p(p+q)}{(p+q)(p+q)(p-q)}$ Multiply for LCD.

$\dfrac{(p+q)(3p-q)}{(p+q)(p+q)(p-q)}$ Add.

$\dfrac{3p-q}{p^2-q^2}$ Simplify.

MULTIPLYING AND DIVIDING RATIONAL EXPRESSIONS

Rational expressions (having the same denominator) can be **multiplied** and **divided** using the same rules as rational numbers. For multiplication, multiply the numerator by the numerator and the denominator by the denominator. To divide, multiply by the reciprocal. Always simplify the answer.

Example 1:

$$\frac{x^2 + 3x}{x^2 + 2x - 3} \cdot \frac{x+1}{x}$$

$$\frac{x(x+3)(x+1)}{x(x+3)(x-1)} \qquad \text{Multiply.}$$

$$\frac{x+1}{x-1} \qquad \text{Simplify.}$$

Example 2:

$$\frac{7x^2}{3} \div \frac{14x^2}{6}$$

$$\frac{7x^2}{3} \cdot \frac{6}{14x^2} \qquad \text{Multiply by reciprocal.}$$

$$= 1 \qquad \text{Simplify}$$

15. LINEAR EQUATIONS AND INEQUALITIES.

15.1 LINEAR EQUATIONS AND INEQUALITIES in ONE VARIABLE

A **linear equation in one variable** can be written in the form $ax + b = 0$, where a + b are real numbers and a ≠ 0.

An equation can be solved by performing the same operations on both sides of the equation.

Example:

$$4x - 3 = {}^-5x + 6$$
$$(4x - 3) + 3 = ({}^-5x + 6) + 3 \qquad \text{Add 3.}$$
$$4x = {}^-5x + 9 \qquad \text{Simplify.}$$
$$4x + 5x = ({}^-5x + 9) + 5x \qquad \text{Add } 5x.$$
$$\frac{9x}{9} = \frac{9}{9} \qquad \text{Simplify.}$$
$$\qquad\qquad\qquad \text{Divide by 9.}$$
$$x = 1 \qquad \text{Simplify.}$$

To **check**, substitute the solution in the original equation.

$$4x - 3 = {}^-5x + 6$$
$$4(1) - 3 \ ? \ {}^-5(1) + 6$$
$$1 = 1$$

An **inequality** is a statement that two expressions are *not* equal. The symbols used are < (less than), > (greater than), ≤ (less than or equal to), ≥ (greater than or equal to) and ≠ (not equal to). Most inequalities have an infinite number of solutions. Methods for solving inequalities are similar to those used for solving equations, with this exception. When both sides of an inequality are multiplied or divided by a <u>negative</u> real number, the inequality sign in reversed.

Example 1:

$$3x - 2 > 13$$

$$(3x - 2) + 2 > 13 + 2 \qquad \text{Add 2.}$$

$$\frac{3x}{3} > \frac{15}{3} \qquad \text{Simplify.}$$

$$\qquad\qquad\qquad \text{Divide by 3.}$$

$$x > 5 \qquad \text{Simplify.}$$

Thus the solution set is all real numbers greater than 5.

Example 2:

$$x + 11 \leq 5x + 3$$

$$(x + 11) - 11 \leq (5x + 3) - 11 \qquad \text{Subtract 11.}$$

$$x \leq 5x - 8 \qquad \text{Simplify.}$$

$$x - 5x \leq 5x - 8 - 5x \qquad \text{Subtract } 5x.$$

$$\frac{-4x}{-4} \leq \frac{-8}{-4} \qquad \text{Simplify.}$$

$$\qquad\qquad\qquad \text{Divide by -4.}$$

$$x \geq 2 \qquad \text{Reverse the inequality sign.}$$

Thus the solution set is all real numbers greater than or equal to 2.

15.2   LINEAR EQUATIONS WITH ABSOLUTE VALUES

The **absolute value** of a real number is the positive value of that number.
$|x| = x$ when $x \geq 0$ and
$|x| = -x$ when $x < 0$.

Examples: $|7| = 7$ $|-13| = 13$

To <u>solve</u> linear equations with absolute value, derive <u>two</u> equations.
If $|x| = n$, then $x = n$ or $x = -n$

Example 1: $|y - 7| = 2$

$y - 7 = 2$	or	$y - 7 = -2$
$y = 9$	or	$y = 5$

The solutions must be checked.

$|y - 7| = 2$	$|y - 7| = 2$
$|9 - 7|\ ?\ 2$	$|5 - 7|\ ?\ 2$
$|2|\ ?\ 2$	$|-2|\ ?\ 2$
$2 = 2$	$2 = 2$
true	true

isolate 11

Example 2: $|3x| + 4 = x$

$|3x| = x - 4$

$3x = x - 4$	or	$3x = -(x - 4)$
$2x = -4$	or	$3x = -x + 4$
		$4x = 4$
$x = -2$	or	$x = 1$

The solutions must be checked.

$|3x| + 4 = -2$	$|3x| + 4 = 1$
$|3 \cdot -2| + 4\ ?\ -2$	$|3 \cdot 1| + 4\ ?\ 1$
$|-6| + 4\ ?\ -2$	$|3| + 4\ ?\ 1$
$6 + 4\ ?\ -2$	$3 + 4\ ?\ 1$
$10 \neq -2$	$7 \neq 1$

Since no solution is true, the solution set is empty.

An **inequality with absolute value** can be solved in a similar manner to an equation. Further, for r > 0 (where r is a positive real number)

$$\text{if } |x| < r \quad \text{then} \quad -r < x < r$$
$$\text{and if } |x| > r \quad \text{then} \quad x < -r \ or \ x > r$$

<u>Example 1</u>: $\quad |x - 1| < 4$

$$x - 1 < 4 \qquad or \qquad x - 1 > -4$$
$$x < 5 \qquad or \qquad x > -3$$

Thus the solution set is all real numbers between -3 and 5.

To **check**, choose a random value in the solution set.

If $x = -1$ $\quad$ then $\quad |x - 1| < 4$

$$|-1 - 1| < 4$$
$$|-2| < 4$$
$$2 < 4 \quad \text{true}$$

<u>Example 2</u>: $\quad |4 + x| - 3 \geq 0$

$$|4 + x| \geq 3$$
$$4 + x \geq 3 \qquad or \qquad 4 + x \leq -3$$
$$x \geq -1 \qquad or \qquad x \leq -7$$

The solution set is all real number less than -7 or greater than -1.

To check, choose two random values in the solution set.

If $x = 4$ $\quad |4 + x| - 3 \geq 0$ $\qquad and \qquad$ If $x = -9$ $\quad |4 + x| - 3 \geq 0$

$$|4 + 4| - 3 \geq 0 \qquad\qquad\qquad |4 - 9| - 3 \geq 0$$
$$|8| - 3 \geq 0 \qquad\qquad\qquad\quad |-5| - 3 \geq 0$$
$$8 - 3 \geq 0 \qquad\qquad\qquad\quad 5 - 3 \geq 0$$
$$5 \geq 0 \qquad\qquad\qquad\qquad 2 \geq 0$$
$$\text{true} \qquad\qquad\qquad\qquad\quad \text{true}$$

16. SOLVING PAIRS OF LINEAR EQUATIONS.

The solution set of a **pair of linear equations** is all the ordered pairs of real numbers that satisfy both equations, thus the intersection of the lines (see competency 17).

Equivalent or **dependent** equations are two equations that are represented by the same line; that is, one is a multiple of the other.

Example: $3x - 4y = 8$
$6x - 8y = 16$

Consistent equations are pairs of equations to which we can find a solution.

Example: $x + 3y = 5$
$2x - y = 15$

Inconsistent equations can be represented by parallel lines; that is, there are no values of x and y that satisfy both equations.

Example: $2x - y = 3$
$6x - 3y = 2$

There are two methods for **solving linear equations:**
linear combinations and substitution.

In the **substitution** method, an equation is solved for either variable. Then, that solution is substituted in the other equation to find the remaining variable.

Example:

(1) $\quad 2x + 8y = 4$
(2) $\quad x - 3y = 5$

(2a) $\quad x = 3y + 5$ $\qquad$ Solve equation (2) for x

(1a) $\quad 2(3y + 5) + 8y = 4$ $\qquad$ Substitute x in equation (1)
$\qquad 6y + 10 + 8y = 4$ $\qquad$ Solve.
$\qquad\qquad\qquad 14y = -6$
$\qquad\qquad\qquad\quad y = \frac{-3}{7}$ $\qquad$ Solution

(2) $\quad x - 3y = 5$
$\qquad x - 3(\frac{-3}{7}) = 5$ $\qquad$ Substitute the value of y.
$\qquad x = \frac{26}{7} = 3\frac{5}{7}$ $\qquad$ Solution

Thus the solution set of the system of equations is $(3\frac{5}{7}, \frac{-3}{7})$.

In the **linear combinations** method, one or both of the equations are replaced with an equivalent equation in order that the two equations can be combined (added or subtracted) to eliminate one variable.

Example 1: Find the solution set.

$$(1) \quad 4x + 3y = -2$$
$$(2) \quad 5x - y = 7$$

$$(1) \quad 4x + 3y = -2$$
$$(2a) \quad 15x - 3y = 21 \qquad \text{Multiply equation (2) by 3}$$

$$19x = 19 \qquad \text{Combining (1) and (2a)}$$
$$x = 1 \qquad \text{Solve.}$$

To find y, substitute the value of x in equation 1 (or 2).

$$(1) \quad 4x + 3y = -2$$
$$4(1) + 3y = -2$$
$$4 + 3y = -2$$
$$3y = -2$$
$$y = -2$$

Thus the solution is $x = 1$ and $y = -2$ or the order pair (1, -2).

Example 2: Find the solution set.

$$(1) \quad 3x + 3y = 2$$
$$(2) \quad 5x - 2y = 1$$

$$(1a) \quad 6x + 6y = 4 \qquad \text{Multiply equation (1) by 2}$$
$$(2a) \quad 15x - 6y = 3 \qquad \text{Multiply equation (2) by 3}$$

$$21x = 7 \qquad \text{Adding equations (1a) and (2a)}$$

$$x = \tfrac{1}{3} \qquad \text{Solve.}$$

$$(1) \quad 3x + 3y = 2$$
$$3(\tfrac{1}{3}) + 3y = 2 \qquad \text{Substitute the value of } x \text{ in (1)}$$
$$1 + 3y = 2$$
$$3y = 1$$
$$y = \tfrac{1}{3}$$

Thus, the solution of the system of equations is $(\tfrac{1}{3}, \tfrac{1}{3})$.

17 GRAPHING

17.1 GRAPHING ON THE NUMBER LINE

When graphing a first degree equation, solve for the variable. The graph of this solution will be a single point on the number line. There will be no arrows.

When graphing a linear inequality, the dot will be hollow if the inequality sign is < or >. If the inequality signs is either $\geq$ or $\leq$, the dot on the graph will be solid. The arrow goes to the right for $\geq$ or >. The arrow goes to the left for < or $\leq$.

Example 1: $5(x + 2) + 2x = 3(x - 2)$
$5x + 10 + 2x = 3x - 6$
$7x + 10 = 3x - 6$
$4x = -16$
$x = -4$

Example 2: $2(3x - 7) > 10x - 2$
$6x - 14 > 10x - 2$
$-4x > 12$
$x < -3$

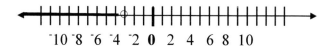

17.2 GRAPHING LINEAR EQUATIONS AND INEQUALITIES

A first degree equation can be written in the form $ax + by = c$. To graph this equation, find either one point and the slope of the line or find two points. To find a point and slope, solve the equation for y. This gets the equation in the **slope-intercept form**, $y = mx + b$. The point $(0,b)$ is the y-intercept and m is the line's slope.

To find two points, substitute any number for x, then solve for y. Repeat this with a different number. To find the intercepts, substitute 0 for x and then 0 for y.

Remember that graphs will go up as they go to the right when the slope is positive. Negative slopes make the lines go down as they go to the right.

If the equation solves to $x = $ a constant, then the graph is a **vertical line**. It only has an x- intercept. Its slope is undefined.

If the equation solves to $y = $ a constant, then the graph is a **horizontal line**. It only has a y-intercept. Its slope is 0 (zero).

When graphing a linear inequality, the line will be dotted if the inequality sign is $<$ or $>$. If the inequality signs are either $\leq$ or $\geq$, the line on the graph will be a solid line.
Shade above the line when the inequality sign is $>$ or $\geq$. Shade below the line when the inequality sign is $<$ or $\leq$. For inequalities of the form $x > k$, $x \geq k$, $x < k$, or $x \leq k$ where k = any number, the graph will be a vertical line (solid or dotted.) Shade to the right for $>$ or $\geq$. Shade to the left for $<$ or $\leq$.
Remember: Dividing or multiplying by a negative number will reverse the direction of the inequality sign.

Examples:

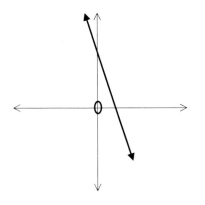

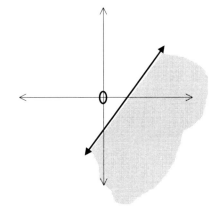

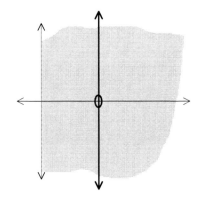

$5x + 2y = 6$
$y = -\frac{5}{2}x + 3$

$3x - 2y \geq 6$
$y \leq \frac{3}{2}x - 3$

$3x + 12 > -3$
$x > -5$

17.3 SLOPE AND THE X- AND Y-INTERCEPTS

A first degree equation has an equation of the form $ax + by = c$. To find the slope of the line, solve the equation for y. This gets the equation into **slope-intercept form**, $y = mx + b$ where represents the slope of the line.

To find the y-intercept, substitute 0 for x and solve for y. This is the y-intercept. The y-intercept is also the value of b in $y = mx + b$.

To find the x-intercept, substitute 0 for y and solve for x. This is the x-intercept.

Example 1: Find the slope and y-intercept of $3x + 2y = 14$.

$$3x + 2y = 14$$
$$2y = -3x + 14$$
$$y = -\tfrac{3}{2}x + 7$$

The slope of the line is $-\tfrac{3}{2}$, the value of m.

The y-intercept of the line is 7.

The intercepts can also be found by substituting 0 in place of the other variabe in the equation.

Example 2: Find the x- and y-intercepts of $3x + 2y = 14$.

To find the y-intercept, let $x = 0$
$$3(0) + 2y = 14$$
$$0 + 2y = 14$$
$$2y = 14$$
$$y = 7$$
(0,7) is the y intercept.

To find the x-intercept: let $y = 0$
$$3x + 2(0) = 14$$
$$3x + 0 = 14$$
$$3x = 14$$
$$x = \tfrac{14}{3}$$
$(\tfrac{14}{3}, 0)$ is the x-intercept.

17.4 WRITING THE EQUATION OF A LINE FROM ITS GRAPH

The equation of a line from its graph can be found by determining its slope and its y-intercept. To find the slope, find two points on the graph where the coordinates are integer values. Using points (x_1, y_1) and (x_2, y_2)

$$\text{slope} = \frac{y_2 - y_1}{x_2 - x_1}$$

or the change in y divided by the change in x

The y-intercept is the y-coordinate of the point where the line crosses the y-axis. The equation can be written in slope-intercept form, which is $y = \mathbf{m}x + \mathbf{b}$, where m is the slope and b is the y-intercept. To re-write the equation into some other form, multiply each term by the common denominator of all the fractions. Then rearrange terms as necessary.

If the graph is a **vertical line**, then the equation solves to
    $x =$ the x coordinate of any point on the line.

If the graph is a **horizontal line**, then the equation solves to
    $y =$ the y coordinate of any point on the line.

18. SOLVING WORD PROBLEMS WITH EQUATIONS

18.1   ONE VARIABLE

An equation may often offer a simple solution to a word problem.

<u>Example</u>: Mark and Mike are twins. Three times Mark's age plus four equals four times Mike's age minus 14. How old are the boys?

Since the boys are twins, their ages are the same. "Translate" the English into Algebra.

Let x = their age

$3x + 4 = 4x - 14$

$18 = x$

The boys are each 18 years old.

18.2   TWO VARIABLES

There may be times when it is necessary or easier to write two equations in two variables to solve a word problem.

<u>Example</u>: The sum of two numbers is 48. One number is three times the other. Find the numbers.

Let x = smaller number
   y = larger number

$x + y = 48$
$y = 3x$

Solve the linear equations by substitution.

$x + 3x = 48$
  $4x = 48$
   $x = 12$ so $y = 36$

The numbers are 12 and 36.

19. ALGEBRAIC RELATIONS and FUNCTIONS

A **relation** is any set of ordered pairs.

The **domain** of a relation is the set which includes all the first coordinates of the ordered pairs.

The **range** of a relation is the set containing all the second coordinates of the ordered pairs.

A **function** is a relation in which different ordered pairs have different first coordinates. (No x values are repeated.)

A **mapping** is a diagram with arrows drawn from each element of the domain to the corresponding elements of the range. If two or more arrows are drawn from the same element of the domain, then it is not a function.

On a graph, use the **vertical line test** to look for a function. If any vertical line intersects the graph of a relation in more than one point, then the relation is not a function.

Example: Determine the domain and range of this mapping.

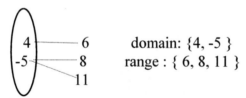

domain: {4, -5 }

range : { 6, 8, 11 }

This is not a function since the x value of -5 can have a y value of both 8 and 11.

20. FACTORING

20.1 MONOMIAL FACTORS

A monomial can be written as the expression ax^n where a is the cooefficient, x is the variable and n is the degree. The cooeficient must be a real number (not equal to zero) and the degree must be a non-negative integer.

To factor out the greatest common factor (GCF), find the GCF of the cooeficients. Then factor out the greatest degree of each variable. Check by multiplying.

Example:
Factor $36x^4y + 18x^3y^3 - 9x^2y^6$
$$9x^2y(4x^2 + 2xy^2 - y^5)$$

Always factor out any monomial factors before factoring further.

20.2 DIFFERENCE OF TWO SQUARES

For a binomial (2 terms), check to see if the expression is the difference of two perfect squares. If both terms are perfect squares, then it factors this way:

$$a^2 - b^2 = (a - b)(a + b)$$

Example:
Factor $4x^2 - 25y^2$
$(2x - 5y)(2x + 5y)$

Note: The sum of two squares can <u>not</u> be factored.

20.3 PERFECT SQUARE TRINOMIALS

A perfect square trinomial can be factored as $x^2 + 2xy + y^2 = (x+y)^2$
and $x^2 - 2xy + y^2 = (x-y)^2$

Example:
Factor $x^2 - 14x + 49$
$(x-7)^2$

20.4 QUADRATIC TRINOMIALS

A quadratic trinomial is an expression in the form $ax^2 + bx + c$. It can be factored into two binomials.

If the constant term, c, is positive, then the factors will look like (+)(+)
$$\text{or } (-)(-)$$
The signs will be positive if the middle term, b, is positive and negative if b is negative .

If the constant term is negative, then the factors will look like (+)(-)
$$\text{or } (-)(+)$$

Find the appropriate factors of the first and last terms that combine
(adding if c is positive and subtracting if c is negative) to equal the middle term.

Example 1:
Factor $x^2 + 7x + 12$
Parentheses (+)(+)
Factors of 12 are 1, 12
         2, 7
         3, 4
The sum of 3 and 4 is 7 so $(x + 3)(x + 4) = x^2 + 7x + 12$

Example 2:
Factor $x^2 - 3x - 40$
Parentheses (+)(-)
Factors of 40 are 1, 40
         2, 20
         4, 10
         5, 8
The difference of 5 and 8 is 3 so $(x + 5)(x - 8) = x^2 - 3x - 40$

Example 3:
Factor $6x^2 - 2x - 8$
GCF = 2 $2(3x^2 - x - 4)$
Parentheses (+)(-)
Factors of 3 are 1, 3
Factors of 4 are 1, 4
         2,2
Arranging these factors so their products combine to equal -4
$(3x - 4)(x + 1) = 3x^2 - x - 4$ and
$2(3x - 4)(x + 1) = 6x^2 - 2x - 8$

20.5 GROUPING

Sometimes an expression may not have one common factor. However, there may be common factors for some of the terms.

Example:

Factor $ax + ay + bx + by$
$(ax + ay) + (bx + by)$
$a(x + y) + b(x + y)$
$(a + b)(x + y)$

20.6 SUM OR DIFFERENCE OF TWO CUBES

A binomial is the sum or difference of two cubes if both terms are perfect cubes.
It can be factored as $a^3 + b^3 = (a + b)(a^2 - ab + b^2)$ and
$$a^3 - b^3 = (a - b)(a^2 + ab + b^2)$$

To factor the sum or difference of perfect cubes, follow this procedure:

a. Factor out any greatest common factor (GCF)
b. Make a parentheses for a binomial (two terms) followed by a trinomial (3 terms).
c. The sign in the first parentheses is the same as the sign in the problem.. The
difference of cubes will have a negative sign in the binomial. The sum of cubes will have
a positive sign in the first parentheses.
d. The first sign in the second parentheses is the opposite of the sign in the first
parentheses. The second sign of the trinomial will always be positive.
e. Determine what would be cubed to equal each term of the problem. Put those
expressions in the first parentheses.
f. To make the three terms of the trinomial, think "square - product -square." Looking at
the binomial, find the product of the two terms, ignoring the signs. This is the trinomial's
second term. Looking at the binomial, square the third term. This is the trinomial's third
term. Except in rare instances, the trinomial does not factor again.

Example 1:
Factor $16x^3 + 54y^3$
$2(8x^3 + 27y^3)$ GCF
$2(\ +\ )(\ -\ +\ )$ signs
$2(\ 2x + 3y)(\ -\ +\ )$ what is cubed to equal $8x^3$ and $27y^3$
$2(\ 2x + 3y)\ (4x^2 - 6xy + 9y^2)$ square - product - square

Example 2:
Factor $64a^3 - 125b^3$
$(\ -\ )(\ +\ +\ )$ signs
$(4a - 5b)(\ +\ +\ )$ what is cubed to equal $64a^3$ and $125b^3$
$(4a - 5b)\ (16a^2 + 20ab + 25b^2)$ square - product - square

Example 3:
$x^3 - 8y^3 = (x - 2y)(x^2 + 2xy + 4y^2)$ difference

Example 4:
$64a^3 + 27b^3 = (4a + 3b)(16a^2 - 12ab + 9b^2)$ sum

21. RATIONAL EXPRESSIONS

21.1 SIMPLIFYING RADICALS

To simplify a radical, follow these steps:

Factor the number or coefficient completely.

For **square roots**, group like factors inpairs. For cube roots, arrange like factors in groups of three. For n[th] roots, group like factors in groups of n.

For each of these groups, put one of that number outside the radical. Any factors that cannot be combined in groups should be multiplied together and left inside the radical.

The index number of a radical is the little number on the front of the radical. For a cube root, the index is 3. If no index appears, then the index is 2 for square roots.

For variables inside the radical, divide the index number of the radical into each exponent. The quotient (the answer to the division) is the new exponent to be written on the variable outside the radical. The remainder from the division is the new exponent on the variable remaining inside the radical sign. If the remainder is zero, then the variable no longer appears in the radical sign.

Note: Remember that the square root of a negative number can be designated by replacing the negative sign inside that square root with an "*i*" in front of the radical (to signify an imaginary number). Then simplify the remaining positive radical by the normal method. Include the *i* outside the radical as part of the answer.

If the index number is an odd number, you can still simplify the radical to get a negative solution.

Example 1:
$$\sqrt{50a^4b^7} = \sqrt{5 \cdot 5 \cdot 2 \cdot a^4 b^7} = 5a^2b^3\sqrt{2b}$$

Example 2:
$$7x\sqrt[3]{16x^5} = 7x\sqrt[3]{2 \cdot 2 \cdot 2 \cdot 2 \cdot x^5} = 7x \cdot 2x\sqrt[3]{2x^2} = 14x^2\sqrt[3]{2x^2}$$

21.2 SIMPLIFYING RATIONAL EXPRESSIONS

Rational expressions can be changed into other equivalent fractions by reducing. When dividing any number of terms by a single term, divide or reduce their coefficients. Then subtract the exponent of a variable in the denominator from the exponent of the same variable in the numerator.

To reduce a rational expression with more than one term in the denominator, the expression must be factored first. Factors that are exactly the same will cancel and each becomes a 1. Factors that have exactly the opposite signs of each other, such as (a - b) and (b - a), will cancel and one factor becomes a 1 and the other becomes a -1.

Example 1:
Simplify
$$\frac{24x^3y^6z^3}{8x^2y^2z} = 3xy^4z^2$$

Example 2:
Simplify
$$\frac{3x^2 - 14xy - 5y^2}{x^2 - 25y^2} = \frac{(3x + y)(x - 5y)}{(x + 5y)(x - 5y)} = \frac{3x + y}{x + 5y}$$

21.3 OPERATIONS WITH RATIONAL EXPRESSIONS

In order to **add or subtract** rational expressions, they must have a common denominator. If they don't have a common denominator, then factor the denominators to determine what factors are missing from each denominator to make the LCD. Multiply both the numerator and the denominator by the missing factor(s). Once the fractions have a common denominator, add or subtract their numerators, but keep the common denominator the same. Factor the numerator if possible and reduce if there are any factors that can be canceled.

In order to **multiply** rational expressions, they do not have to have a common denominator, If you factor each numerator and denominator, you can divide by any common factor that occurs in both the numerator and denominator. Then multiply the remaining factors of the numerator together. Similarly, multiply the remaining factors of the denominator together.

In order to **divide** rational expressions, the problem must be re-written as the first fraction multiplied times the reciprocal of the second fraction. Once the problem has been written as multiplication, factor each numerator and denominator. Continue by folloing the same procedure as multiplication.

Example 1: $\dfrac{5}{x^2-9} - \dfrac{2}{x^2+4x+3} = \dfrac{5}{(x-3)(x+3)} - \dfrac{2}{(x+3)(x-1)} = $ ✗

$$\dfrac{5(x+1)}{(x-3)(x+3)(x+1)} - \dfrac{2(x-3)}{(x-3)(x+1)(x-3)} = \dfrac{5x+5-2x+6}{(x-3)(x+3)(x+1)}$$

$$\dfrac{3x+11}{(x-3)(x+3)(x+1)}$$

Example 2: $\dfrac{x^2-2x-24}{x^2+6x+8} \bullet \dfrac{x^2+3x+2}{x^2-13x+42} = $

$$\dfrac{(x-6)(x+4)}{(x+4)(x+2)} \bullet \dfrac{(x+2)(x+1)}{(x-7)(x-6)} = $$

$$\dfrac{x+1}{x-7}$$

SQUARE ROOTS

Before you can **add or subtract** square roots, the numbers or expressions inside the radicals must be the same. First, simplify the radicals, if possible. If the numbers or expressions inside the radicals are the same, add or subtract the numbers (or like expressions) in front of the radicals. Keep the expression inside the radical the same. Be sure that the radicals are as simplified as possible.

Note: If the expressions inside the radicals are not the same, and cannot be simplified to become the same, then they can not be combined by addition or subtraction.

To **multiply** two square roots together, follow these steps:
a. Multiply what is outside the radicals together.
b. Multiply what is inside the radicals together.
c. Simplify the radical if possible. Multiply whatever is in front of the radical times the expression that is coming out of the radical.

To **divide** one square root by another, follow these steps:
a. Work separately on what is inside or outside the square root sign.
b. Divide or reduce the coefficients outside the radical.
c. Divide any like variables outside the radical.
d. Divide or reduce the coefficients inside the radical.
e. Divide any like variables inside the radical.
f. If there is still a radical in the denominator, multiply both the numerator and denominator by the radical in the denominator. Simplify both resulting radicals and reduce again outside the radical (if possible).

Example 1:
Simplify: $6\sqrt{7} + 2\sqrt{5} + 3\sqrt{7} = 9\sqrt{7} + 2\sqrt{5}$ These can't be combined.

Example 2:
Simplify: $5\sqrt{12} + \sqrt{48} - 2\sqrt{75}$

$$5\sqrt{2\cdot2\cdot3} + \sqrt{2\cdot2\cdot2\cdot2\cdot3} - 2\sqrt{3\cdot5\cdot5}$$
$$5\cdot2\sqrt{3} + 2\cdot2\sqrt{3} - 2\cdot5\sqrt{3}$$
$$10\sqrt{3} + 4\sqrt{3} - 10\sqrt{3} = 4\sqrt{3}$$

21.4 SOLVING RADICAL EQUATIONS

To solve a radical equation, follow these steps:
a. Get the radical alone on one side of the equation.
b. Raise both sides of the equation to the power equal to the index number. Do not raise them to that power term by term, but raise the <u>entire side</u> to that power. Combine any like terms.
c. If there is another radical still in the equation, repeat steps a and b. Repeat as necessary until all the radicals are gone.
d. Solve the resulting equation.
e. Once you have found the answer(s), substitute them into the original equation to check. Use only the principal (positive) square root. Sometimes there are solutions that do not check in the original equations. These are extraneous solutions, which are not correct and must be eliminated. If a problem has more that one potential solution, each solution must be checked separately.

Note: What this really means is that you can simply just substitute the answers from any multiple choice test back into the question to determine which answer choice is correct.

<u>Example 1</u>:
$$\sqrt{2x+1} + 7 = x$$
$$\sqrt{2x+1} = x - 7$$
$$(\sqrt{2x+1})^2 = (x-7)^2 \quad \text{both SIDES are squared}$$
$$2x + 1 = x^2 - 14x + 49$$
$$0 = x^2 - 16x + 48$$
$$0 = (x-12)(x-4)$$
$$x = 12, x = 4$$

Check: $\sqrt{2x+1} + 7 = x$ $\qquad \sqrt{2x+1} + 7 = x$
$\qquad \sqrt{2(12)+1} + 7 = 12$ $\qquad \sqrt{2(4)+1} + 7 = 4$
$\qquad \sqrt{25} + 7 = 12$ $\qquad\qquad \sqrt{9} + 7 = 4$
$\qquad\qquad 5 + 7 = 12$ $\qquad\qquad 3 + 7 \neq 4$ Using positive root
Thus 12 is the only solution.

<u>Example 2</u>: $\sqrt{3x+4} = 2\sqrt{x-4}$
$$(\sqrt{3x+4})^2 = (2\sqrt{x-4})^2$$
$$3x + 4 = 4(x-4)$$
$$3x + 4 = 4x - 16$$
$$20 = x \qquad \text{This checks in the original equation.}$$

Example 3: $\sqrt[4]{7x-3} = 3$
$(\sqrt[4]{7x-3})^4 = 3^4$
$7x - 3 = 81$
$7x = 84$
$x = 12$ This checks in the original equation.

Example 4: $\sqrt{x} = -3$
$(\sqrt{x})^2 = (-3)^2$
$x = 9 \Leftarrow$ This does NOT check in the original equation. Since there is no other answer to check, the correct answer is the empty set or the null set or $\varnothing$.

22. QUADRATIC EQUATIONS

SOLVING QUADRATIC EQUATIONS

A quadratic equation is written in the form $ax^2 + bx + c = 0$. When a quadratic equation is factored, at least one of the factors must equal zero.

Example:
Solve the equation
$x^2 + 10x - 24 = 0$
$(x + 12)(x - 2) = 0$ Factor
$x + 12 = 0$ *or* $x - 2 = 0$ Set each factor equal to 0
$x = -12$ $x = 2$ Solve

Check:
$x^2 + 10x - 24 = 0$
$(-12)^2 + 10(-12) - 24 = 0$ $(2)^2 + 10(2) - 24 = 0$
$144 - 120 - 24 = 0$ $4 + 20 - 24 = 0$
$0 = 0$ $0 = 0$

22.1 COMPLETING THE SQUARE

A quadratic equation that cannot be solved by sight factoring can be solved by completing the square.
a.   If the equation is written in the form $ax^2 + bx + c = 0$, move the constant to the right side of the equation $ax^2 + bx = -c$

b. Divide each term by a $\dfrac{ax^2}{a} + \dfrac{bx}{a} = -\dfrac{c}{a}$

c. Multiply the fraction $\dfrac{b}{a}$ by $\dfrac{1}{2}$

d. Square the resulting fraction and add this fraction to both sides of the equation to complete the square.
e. Write the left side as a perfect square.
f. The square root of the left side of the equation will be one of the squares roots of the right side.
g. Solve and check.

Example 1:
Solve the equation
$x^2 - 6x + 8 = 0$
$x^2 - 6x = -8$ Move the constant to the right side
$x^2 - 6x + 9 = -8 + 9$ Add the square of half the cooeficient of x to both sides
$(x - 3)^2 = 1$ Write the left side as a perfect square
$x - 3 = \sqrt{1}$ or $x - 3 = -\sqrt{1}$ Take the square root of both sides
$x - 3 = 1$ $x - 3 = -1$ Solve
$x = 4$ $x = 2$

Check:
$x^2 - 6x + 8 = 0$
$4^2 - 6(4) + 8 = 0$ $2^2 - 6(2) + 8 = 0$
$16 - 24 + 8 = 0$ $4 - 12 + 8 = 0$
$0 = 0$ $0 = 0$

Example 2:
Solve the equation
$x^2 + 7x + 2 = 0$
$x^2 + 7x = -2$
$x^2 + 7x + \frac{49}{4} = -2 + \frac{49}{4}$
$(x + \frac{7}{2})^2 = \frac{41}{4}$
$x + \frac{7}{2} = \sqrt{\frac{41}{4}}$ $x + \frac{7}{2} = -\sqrt{\frac{41}{4}}$
$x = -\frac{7}{2} + \frac{\sqrt{41}}{2}$ $x = -\frac{7}{2} - \frac{\sqrt{41}}{2}$

22.2 DERIVE THE QUADRATIC FORMULA

To derive the quadratic formula, complete the square on the quadratic equation.

$ax^2 + bx + c = 0$

$ax^2 + bx = -c$ Move the constant to the right side

$x^2 + \dfrac{bx}{a} = -\dfrac{c}{a}$ Divide each term by a

$x^2 + \dfrac{bx}{a} + \left(\dfrac{b}{2a}\right)^2 = -\dfrac{c}{a} + \dfrac{b^2}{4a^2}$ Add the square of half b

$\left(x + \dfrac{b}{2a}\right)^2 = \dfrac{b^2 - 4ac}{4a^2}$ Write the left side as a perfect square

$x + \dfrac{b}{2a} = \dfrac{\sqrt{b^2 - 4ac}}{2a}$ $x + \dfrac{b}{2a} = \dfrac{-\sqrt{b^2 - 4ac}}{2a}$ Take the square root of both sides

$x = -\dfrac{b}{2a} + \dfrac{\sqrt{b^2 - 4ac}}{2a}$ $x = -\dfrac{b}{2a} - \dfrac{\sqrt{b^2 - 4ac}}{2a}$ Solve

$x = \dfrac{-b \pm \sqrt{b^2 - 4ac}}{2a}$

22.3 SOLVING EQUATIONS USING THE QUADRATIC FORMULA

To solve a quadratic equation using the quadratic formula, be sure that your equation is in the form $ax^2 + bx + c = 0$. Substitute these values into the formula

$$x = \frac{-b \pm \sqrt{b^2 - 4ac}}{2a}$$

Example 1:
Solve the equation $3x^2 = 7 + 2x$
$3x^2 - 2x - 7 = 0$
$a = 3 \quad b = -2 \quad c = -7$

$$x = \frac{-(-2) \pm \sqrt{(-2)^2 - 4(3)(-7)}}{2(3)}$$

$$x = \frac{2 \pm \sqrt{4 + 84}}{6}$$

$$x = \frac{2 \pm \sqrt{88}}{6}$$

$$x = \frac{2 \pm 2\sqrt{22}}{6}$$

$$x = \frac{1 \pm \sqrt{22}}{3}$$

Example 2:
Solve the equation $6x^2 - 11x + 4 = 0$
$a = 6, \quad b = -11, \quad c = 4$

$$x = \frac{11 \pm \sqrt{(^-11)^2 - 4(6)(4)}}{2(6)}$$

$$= \frac{11 \pm \sqrt{121 - 96}}{12}$$

$$= \frac{11 \pm \sqrt{25}}{12}$$

$$= \frac{11 \pm 5}{12}$$

$$x = \frac{16}{12} = \frac{4}{3} \quad \text{and} \quad \frac{6}{12} = \frac{1}{2}$$

22.4 DISCRIMINANT

The **discriminant** is the portion of the quadratic formula which is found under the square root sign; that is $b^2 - 4ac$.

The discriminant can be used to determine the nature of the solution of a quadratic equation.

There are three possibilities:
$b^2 - 4ac > 0$, then there are 2 real roots
$b^2 - 4ac = 0$, then exactly one real root exists
$b^2 - 4ac < 0$. then there are no real roots

23. DIRECT AND INVERSE VARIATIONS

DIRECT VARIATION

A **direct variation** can be expressed by the formula
  $y = kx$ where k is a constant, $k \neq 0$.

Example: If y varies directly as x and $y = -8$ when $x = 4$, find y when $x = 11$

First find the **constant of variation**, k.

$$k = \frac{y}{x} = \frac{^{-}8}{4} = {}^{-}2$$

The write an equation with $k = -2$
  $y = -2(11)$
  $y = -22$

INDIRECT VARIATION

An **indirect variation** can be expressed by the formula
  $xy = k$, where k is a constant, $k \neq 0$.

Example: If y varies inversely as x and $y = 20$ when $x = -4$, find y when $x = 14$

  $k = 20(-4) = -80$
Similarly, write and equations with $k = -80$

$$y = \frac{k}{x}$$

$$y = \frac{^{-}80}{14} = {}^{-}5\frac{5}{7}$$

24.   ARITHMETIC AND GEOMETRIC PROGESSIONS

24.1   FINDING SPECIFIED TERMS

Arithmetic Sequences

When given a set of numbers where the common difference between the terms is constant, use the following formula:

$a_{n} = a_{1+} (n-1)d$

   where a_1 = the first term

   n = the nth term (general term)

   d = the common difference

Example 1:

Find the 8th term of the arithmetic sequence 5, 8, 11, 14, ...

$a_n = a_1 + (n-1)d$	
$a_1 = 5$	identify the 1st term
$d = 8 - 5 = 3$	find d
$a_n = 5 + (8-1)3$	substitute
$a_n = 26$	

Example 2:

Given two terms of an arithmetic sequence, find a_1 and d.

$a_4 = 21$ $a_6 = 32$

$a_n = a + (n-1)d$	$a_4 = 21, n = 4$
$21 = a_1 + (4-1)d$	$a_6 = 32, n = 6$
$32 = a_1 + (6-1)d$	

$21 = a_1 + 3d$	solve the system of equations
$32 = a_1 + 5d$	

$21 = a_1 + 3d$	
$-32 = -a_1 - 5d$	multiply by -1
$-11 = -2d$	add the equations
$5.5 = d$	

$21 = a_1 + 3(5.5)$	substitute d = 5.5, into one of the equations
$21 = a_1 + 16.5$	
$a_1 = 4.5$	

The sequence begins with 4.5 and has a common difference of 5.5 between numbers.

Geometric Sequences

When using geometric sequences, consecutive numbers are compared to find the common ratio.

$r = \dfrac{a_{n+1}}{a_n}$

where r = common ratio
a = the nth term

The ratio is then used in the geometric sequence formula:

$r = a_1{}^{n-1}$

$a_n = a_1 \cdot r^{n-1}$

Example:
Find the 8th term of the geometric sequence 2, 8, 32, 128 ...

$r = \dfrac{a_{n+1}}{a_n}$ use common ratio formula to find ratio

$r = \frac{8}{2}$ substitute $a_n = 2$ $a_{n+1} = 8$

$r = 4$

$a_n = a_1 \cdot r^{n-1}$ use r = 4 to solve for the 8th term
$a_n = 2 \cdot 4^{8-1}$
$a_n = 32{,}768$

24.2 SUM OF TERMS IN A PROGRESSION

The sums of terms in a progression is simply found by determining if it is an arithmetic or geometric sequence and then using the appropriate formula.

Sum of first n terms of $s_n = \frac{n}{2}(a_1 + a_n)$

an Arithmetic Sequence   or $s_n = \frac{n}{2}[2a_1 + (n-1)d]$

Sum of first n terms of $s_n = \dfrac{a_1(n^n - 1)}{r - 1}$, $r \neq 1$

a Geometric Sequence

Example 1:

$\displaystyle\sum_{i=1}^{10}(2i + 2)$ This means find the sum of the terms begining with the first term and

ending with the 10th term of the sequence $a = 2i + 2$

$a_1 = 2(1) + 2 = 4$ find a_1 and a_{10}

$a_{10} = 2(10) + 2 = 22$

$s_n = \frac{n}{2}(a_1 + a_n)$ find sum

$s_{10} = \frac{10}{2}(4 + 22)$ substitute known values

$s_{10} = 130$ solve

Example 2:

Find the sum of the first 6 terms in an arithmetic sequence if the first term is 2 and the common difference is -3.

$n = 6$ $a_1 = 2$ $d = -3$

$s_n = \frac{n}{2}[2a_1 + (n-1)d]$

$s_n = \frac{6}{2}[2\bullet2 + (6-1)(-3)]$ substitute known values

$s_n = 3[4 + (-15)]$ solve

$s_n = 33$ ↑

            means + ?

25. BASIC GEOMETRIC CONCEPTS

25.1 POINTS, LINES, PLANES, AND ANGLES

A point, a line and a plane are actually undefined terms since we cannot give a satisfactory definition using simple defined terms. However, their properties and characteristics give a clear understanding of what they are.

A **point** indicates place or position. It has no length, width or thickness.

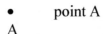
point A

A **line** is considered a set of points. Lines may be straight or curved, but the term line commonly denotes a straight line. Lines extend indefinitely.

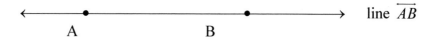
line $\overrightarrow{AB}$

A **plane** is a set of points composing a flat surface. A plane also has no boundaries.

plane A

A **line segment** has two endpoints.

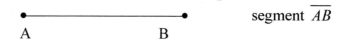
segment $\overline{AB}$

A **ray** has exactly one endpoint. It extend indefinitely in one direction.

ray $\overrightarrow{AB}$

An **angle** is formed by the intersection of two rays.

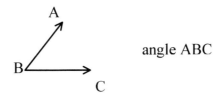

angle ABC

An infinite number of lines can be drawn through any point.

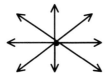

Exactly one line can be drawn through two points.

Two lines intersect at exactly one point.

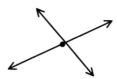

Two planes intersect to form a line.

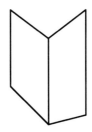

The <u>intersection</u> of two sets of points is those points that belong to <u>both</u> sets.

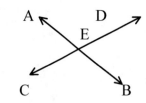

$\overleftrightarrow{AB} \cap \overleftrightarrow{CD} = \{E\}$ Line $\overleftrightarrow{AB}$ intersects line $\overleftrightarrow{CD}$ at point E.

$\overline{AC} \cap \overline{BD} = \overline{BC}$ Segment AC intersects segment BD at segment BC.

The <u>union</u> of two sets of points is those points that belong to <u>either</u> or <u>both</u> sets.

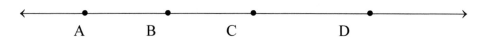

$\overline{AC} \cup \overline{BD} = \overline{AD}$ The union of segment AC and segment BD is segment AD.

25.2 TYPES OF ANGLES

Angles are measured in degrees. $1° = \frac{1}{360}$ of a circle.

A **right angle** measures $90°$.

An **acute angle** measures more than $0°$ and less than $90°$.

An **obtuse angle** measures more than $90°$ and less than $180°$.

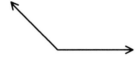

A **straight angle** measures $180°$.

A **reflexive angle** measures more than $180°$ and less than $360°$.

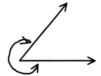

25.3   RELATIONSHIPS BETWEEN ANGLES

Adjacent angles have a common vertex and common side, but do not have any interior points in common.

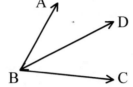

∠ABD and ∠CBD are adjacent angles.

Vertical angles are formed by two intersecting lines.

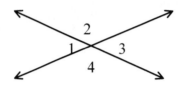

∠1 and ∠3 are vertical angles.
∠2 and ∠4 are vertical angles

Vertical angles have the same measure.

The sum of the measures of **complementary angles** is 90°. Each angle is said to be a complement of the other.

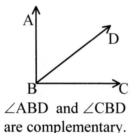

∠ABD and ∠CBD
are complementary.

These angles are complementary, since 28° + 62° = 90°.

The sum of the measures of **supplementary angles** is 180°. Each angle is said to be a supplement of the other.

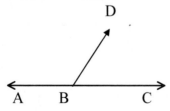

∠ABD and ∠CBD
are supplementary.

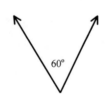 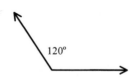

These angles are supplementary, since 60° + 120° = 180°

When two lines are cut by a third line, called a **transversal**, four types of angles are formed.

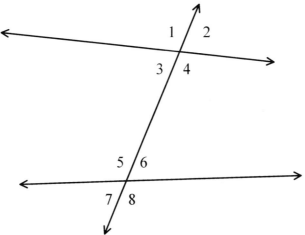

∠1 and ∠4 are **vertical angles**.   ∠2 and ∠3 are **vertical angles**.
∠5 and ∠8 are **vertical angles**.   ∠6 and ∠7 are **vertical angles**.

∠1 and ∠3 are **adjacent angles**.   ∠2 and ∠4 are **adjacent angles**.
∠5 and ∠7 are **adjacent angles**.   ∠6 and ∠8 are **adjacent angles**.

∠1 and ∠5 are **corresponding angles**.   ∠2 and ∠6 are **corresponding angles**.
∠3 and ∠7 are **corresponding angles**.   ∠4 and ∠8 are **corresponding angles**.

∠4 and ∠5 are **alternate interior angles**.   ∠3 and ∠6 are **alternate interior angles**.

∠1 and ∠8 are **alternate exterior angles**.   ∠2 and ∠7 are **alternate exterior angles**.

25.4   LINES AND PLANES

Two lines intersect at exactly one point. Two lines are **perpendicular** if their intersection forms right angles.

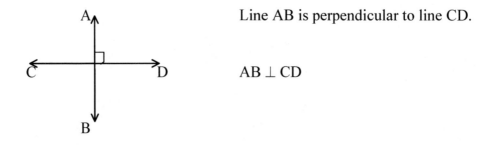

Line AB is perpendicular to line CD.

AB $\perp$ CD

Two lines in the same plane that do not intersect are **parallel**. Parallel lines are everywhere equidistant.

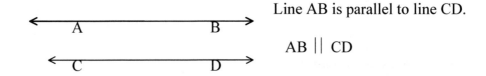

Line AB is parallel to line CD.

AB $\parallel$ CD

Two lines in *different* planes that do not intersect are **skew.**

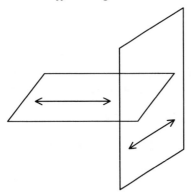

Two planes intersect at exactly one line.

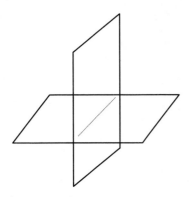

Parallel planes do not intersect .

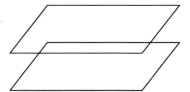

A line and a plane are parallel if they do not intersect.

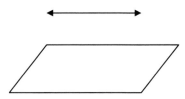

A line and a plane are perpendicular if they intersect and the line is perpendicular to all lines in the plane that pass through the point of intersection.

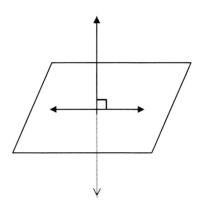

26. POLYGONS

26.1   TRIANGLES

A **triangle** is a polygon with three sides.

Triangles can be classified by the types of angles or the lengths of their sides.

CLASSIFYING BY ANGLES

An **acute** triangle has exactly three *acute* angles.
A **right** triangle has one *right* angle.
An **obtuse** triangle has one *obtuse* angle.

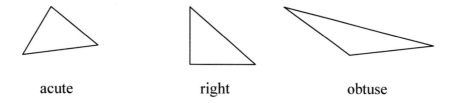

       acute   right   obtuse

CLASSIFYING BY SIDES

All *three* sides of an **equilateral** triangle are the same length.
Two sides of an **isosceles** triangle are the same length.
None of the sides of a **scalene** triangle are the same length.

  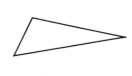

     equilateral   isosceles   scalene

26.2 MEASURING ANGLES OF A TRIANGLE

The sum of the measures of the angles of a triangle is 180°.

Example 1:
Can a triangle have two right angles?
> No. A right angle measures 90°, therefore the sum of two right angles would be 180° and there could not be third angle.

Example 2:
Can a right triangle have two obtuse angles?
> No. Since an obtuse angle measures more than 90° the sum of two obtuse angles would be greater than 180°.

Example 3:
Can a right triangle be obtuse?
> No. Once again, the sum of the angles would be more than 180°.

Example 4:
In a triangle, the measure of the second angle is three times the first. The third angle equals the sum of the measures of the first two angles. Find the number of degrees in each angle.

> Let x = the number of degrees in the first angle
> $3x$ = the number of degrees in the second angle
> $x + 3x$ = the measure of the third angle
> Since the sum of the measures of all three angles is 180°
> $$x + 3x + (x + 3x) = 180$$
> $$8x = 180$$
> $$x = 22.5$$
> $$3x = 67.5$$
> $$x + 3x = 90$$

Thus the angles measure 22.5°, 67.5°, and 90°. Additionally, the triangle is a right triangle.

EXTERIOR ANGLES

Two adjacent angles form a **linear pair** when they have a common side and their remaining sides form a straight angle. Angles in a linear pair are supplementary. An **exterior angle** of a triangle forms a linear pair with an angle of the triangle.

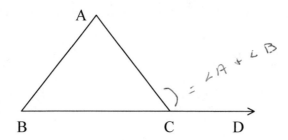

$\angle$ACD is an exterior angle of triangle ABC, forming a linear pair with $\angle$ACB.

The measure of an exterior angle of a triangle is equal to the sum of the measures of the two non-adjacent interior angles.

Example:
In triangle ABC, the measure of $\angle$A is twice the measure of $\angle$B. $\angle$C is 30° more than their sum. Find the measure of the exterior angle formed at $\angle$C.

$\quad$ Let $\quad x$ = the measure of $\angle$B

$\qquad 2x$ = the measure of $\angle$A

$\quad x + 2x + 30$ = the measure of $\angle$C

$\quad x + 2x + x + 2x + 30 = 180$

$\qquad\qquad 6x + 30 = 180$

$\qquad\qquad\quad 6x = 150$

$\qquad\qquad\quad\quad x = 25$

$\qquad\qquad\quad 2x = 50$

It is not necessary to find the measure of the third angle, since the exterior angle equals the sum of the opposite interior angles. Thus the exterior angle at $\angle$C measures 75°.

26.3 and 26.4 ANGLES OF A POLYGON

A **polygon** is a simple closed figure composed of line segments. In a **regular polygon** all sides are the same length and all angles are the same measure.

The sum of the measures of the **interior angles** of a polygon can be determined using the following formula, where n represents the number of angles in the polygon.

Sum of $\angle$s $= 180(n - 2)$

The measure of each angle of a regular polygon can be found by dividing the sum of the measures by the number of angles.

Measure of $\angle = \dfrac{180(n-2)}{n}$

Example: Find the measure of each angle of a regular octagon.
Since an octagon has eight sides, each angle equals

$$\frac{180(8-2)}{8} = \frac{180(6)}{8} = 135°$$

The sum of the measures of the **exterior angles** of a polygon, taken one angle at each vertex, equals $360°$.

The measure of each exterior angle of a regular polygon can be determined using the following formula, where n represents the number of angles in the polygon.

Measure of exterior $\angle$ of regular polygon $= 180 - \dfrac{180(n-2)}{n}$

or, more simply $= \dfrac{360}{n}$

Example: Find the measure of the interior and exterior angles of a regular pentagon.
Since a pentagon has five sides, each exterior angle measures

$$\frac{360}{5} = 72°$$

Since each exterior angles is supplementary to its interior angle, the interior angle measures 180 - 72 or 108°.

26.5 and 26.6 and 26.7   QUADRILATERALS

A **quadrilateral** is a polygon with four sides.
The sum of the measures of the angles of a convex quadrilateral is 360°.

A **trapezoid** is a quadrilateral with exactly <u>one</u> pair of parallel sides.

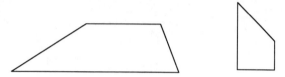

In an **isosceles trapezoid**, the non-parallel sides are congruent.

A **parallelogram** is a quadrilateral with <u>two</u> pairs of parallel sides.

A **rectangle** is a parallelogram with a right angle.

A **rhombus** is a parallelogram with all sides equal length.

A **square** is a rectangle with all sides equal length.

PROPERTIES

A **parallelogram** exhibits these properties.

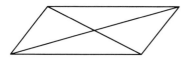

The diagonals bisect each other.
Each diagonal divides the parallelogram into two congruent triangles.
Both pairs of opposite sides are congruent.
Both pairs of opposite angles are congruent.
Two adjacent angles are supplementary.

Example 1:
Find the measures of the other three angles of a parallelogram if one angle measures 38°.

Since opposite angles are equal, there are two angles measuring 38°.
Since adjacent angles are supplementary, 180 - 38 = 142
so the other two angles measure 142° each.

$$\begin{array}{r} 38 \\ 38 \\ 142 \\ + \ 142 \\ \hline 360 \end{array}$$

Example 2:
The measures of two adjacent angles of a parallelogram are $3x + 40$ and $x + 70$.
Find the measures of each angle.

$$2(3x + 40) + 2(x + 70) = 360$$
$$6x + 80 + 2x + 140 = 360$$
$$8x + 220 = 360$$
$$8x = 140$$
$$x = 17.5$$
$$3x + 40 = 92.5$$
$$x + 70 = 87.5$$

Thus the angles measure 92.5°, 92.5°, 87.5°, and 87.5°.

Since a **rectangle** is a special type of parallelogram, it exhibits all the properties of a parallelogram. All the angles of a rectangle are right angles because of congruent opposite angles. Additionally, the diagonals of a rectangle are congruent.

A **rhombus** also has all the properties of a parallelogram. Additionally, its diagonals are perpendicular to each other and they bisect its angles.

A **square** has all the properties of a rectangle <u>and</u> a rhombus.

Example 1:
   True or false?

All squares are rhombuses.	True
All parallelograms are rectangles	False - <u>some</u> parallelograms are rectangles
All rectangles are parallelograms.	True
Some rhombuses are squares.	True
Some rectangles are trapezoids.	False - only <u>one</u> pair of parallel sides
All quadrilaterals are parallelograms.	False -some quadrilaterals are parallelograms
Some squares are rectangles.	False - all squares are rectangles
Some parallelograms are rhombuses.	True

Example 2:
In **rhombus** ABCD side AB = $3x$ - 7 and side CD = x + 15. Find the length of each side.
Since all the sides are the same length, $3x - 7 = x + 15$
$$2x = 22$$
$$x = 11$$
Since $3(11) - 7 = 25$ and $11 + 15 = 25$, each side measures 26 units.

An **isosceles trapezoid** has the following properties:

The diagonals of an isosceles trapezoid are congruent.
The base angles of an isosceles trapezoid are congruent

27. CONGRUENCE

27.1   CONGRUENT POLYGONS

Congruent figures have the same size and shape. If one is placed above the other, it will fit exactly. Congruent lines have the same length. Congruent angles have equal measures.

The symbol for congruent is $\cong$.

Polygons (pentagons) ABCDE and VWXYZ are congruent. They are exactly the same size and shape.

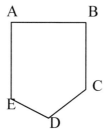 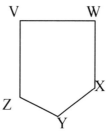

$$ABCDE \cong VWXYZ$$

Corresponding parts are those congruent angles and congruent sides, that is

corresponding angles	*corresponding sides*
$\angle A \leftrightarrow \angle V$	AB $\leftrightarrow$ VW
$\angle B \leftrightarrow \angle W$	BC $\leftrightarrow$ WX
$\angle C \leftrightarrow \angle X$	CD $\leftrightarrow$ XY
$\angle D \leftrightarrow \angle Y$	DE $\leftrightarrow$ YZ
$\angle E \leftrightarrow \angle Z$	AE $\leftrightarrow$ VZ

27.2   CONGRUENT TRIANGLES

Two triangles can be proven congruent by comparing pairs of appropriate congruent corresponding parts.

SSS POSTULATE

If three sides of one triangle are congruent to three sides of another triangle, then the two triangles are congruent.

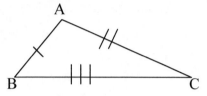 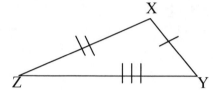

Since AB ≅ XY, BC ≅ YZ and AC ≅ XZ, then ΔABC ≅ Δ XYZ.

<u>Example</u>: Given isosceles triangle ABC with D the midpoint of base AC, prove the two triangles formed by BD are congruent.

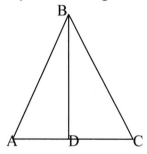

Proof:
1. Isosceles triangle ABC, D midpoint of base AC   Given
2. AB ≅ BC   An isosceles Δ has two congruent
                                                     sides
3. AD ≅ DC   Midpoint divides a triangle into two
                                                     equal parts
4. BD ≅ BD   Reflexive
5. Δ ABD ≅ ΔBCD   SSS

SAS POSTULATE

If two sides and the included angle of one triangle are congruent to two sides and the included angle of another triangle, then the two triangles are congruent.

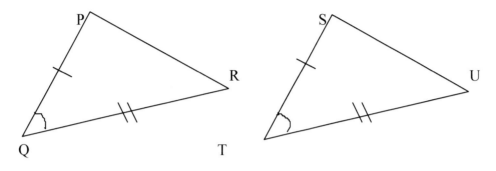

Example:

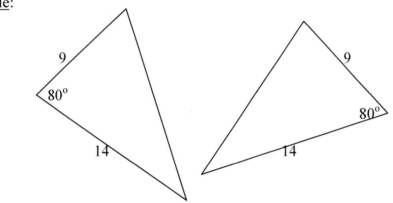

The two triangles are congruent by SAS.

ASA POSTULATE

If two angles and the included side of one triangle are congruent to two angles and the included side of another triangle, the triangles are congruent.

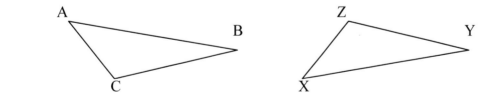

$\angle A \cong \angle X$, $\angle B \cong \angle Y$, $AB \cong XY$ then $\triangle ABC \cong \triangle XYZ$ by ASA

Example 1: Given two right triangles with one leg of each measuring 6 cm and the adjacent angle 37°, prove the triangles are congruent.

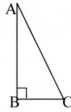 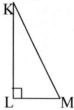

1. Right triangles ABC and KLM
   AB = KL = 6 cm
   $\angle A = \angle K = 37°$
	Given

2. AB ≅ KL $\angle A \cong \angle K$	Figures with the same measure are congruent
3. $\angle B \cong \angle L$	All right angles are congruent.
4. $\triangle ABC \cong \triangle KLM$	ASA

Example 2:
What method would you use to prove the triangles congruent?

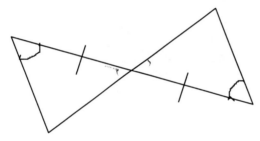

ASA because vertical angles are congruent.

27.3   CONGRUENT TRIANGLES

AAS THEOREM

If two angles and a non-included side of one triangle are congruent to the corresponding parts of another triangle, then the triangles are congruent.

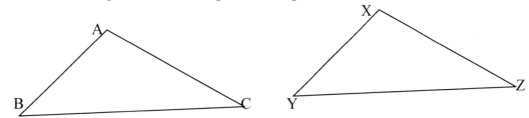

$\angle B \cong \angle Y$, $\angle C \cong \angle Z$, AC$\cong$XZ, then $\triangle ABC \cong \triangle XYZ$ by AAS.

We can derive this theorem because if two angles of the triangles are congruent, then the third angle must also be congruent. Therefore, we can uses the ASA postulate.

HL THEOREM

If the hypotenuse and a leg of one right triangle are congruent to the corresponding parts of another right triangle, the triangles are congruent.

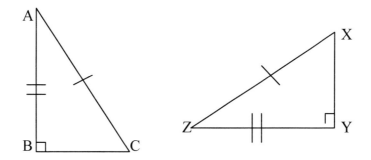

Since $\angle B$ and $\angle Y$ are right angles and AC $\cong$ XZ (hypotenuse of each triangle), AB $\cong$ YZ (corresponding leg of each triangle), then $\triangle ABC \cong \triangle XYZ$ by HL.

<u>Example</u>: What method would you use to prove the triangles congruent?

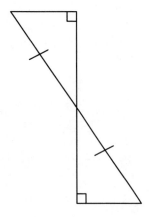

AAS

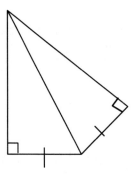

HL

28.   SIMILAR POLYGONS

Two figures that have the **same shape** are **similar**. Two polygons are similar if corresponding angles are congruent and corresponding sides are in proportion. Corresponding parts of similar polygons are proportional.

Example: Given two similar quadrilaterals. Find the lengths of sides x, y, and z.

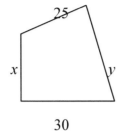 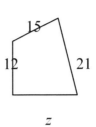

Since corresponding sides are proportional, $\dfrac{15}{25} = \dfrac{3}{5}$ so the scale is $\dfrac{3}{5}$

$$\frac{12}{x} = \frac{3}{5}$$ $$\frac{21}{y} = \frac{3}{5}$$ $$\frac{z}{30} = \frac{3}{5}$$

$$3x = 60$$ $$3y = 105$$ $$5z = 90$$
$$x = 20$$ $$y = 35$$ $$z = 18$$

SIMILAR TRIANGLES

AA Similarity Postulate
If two angles of one triangle are congruent to two angles of another triangle, then the triangles are similar.

SAS Similarity Theorem
If an angle of one triangle is congruent to an angle of another triangle and the sides including those angles are in proportion, then the triangles are similar.

SSS Similarity Theorem
If the sides of two triangles are in proportion, then the triangles are similar.

Example:

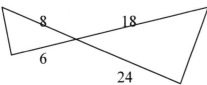

The two triangles are similar since the sides are proportional and vertical angles are congruent.

29. RIGHT TRIANGLES

29.1 ALTITUDE TO THE HYPOTENUSE

A **right triangle** is a triangle with one right angle. The side opposite the right angle is called the **hypotenuse**. The other two sides are the **legs**. An **altitude** is a line drawn from one vertex, perpendicular to the opposite side.

When an altitude is drawn to the hypotenuse of a right triangle, then the two triangles formed are similar to the original triangle and to each other.

Example:

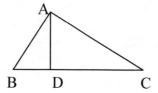

Given right triangle ABC with right angle at A, altitude AD drawn to hypotenuse BD at D.

$\triangle ABC \sim \triangle ABD \sim \triangle ACD$ The triangles formed are similar to each other and to the original right triangle.

29.2   GEOMETRIC MEAN

If *a, b* and *c* are positive numbers such that $\dfrac{a}{b} = \dfrac{b}{c}$

then *b* is called the **geometric mean** between *a* and *c*.

Example:
Find the geometric mean between 6 and 30.

$$\frac{6}{x} = \frac{x}{30}$$
$$x^2 = 180$$
$$x = \sqrt{180} = \sqrt{36 \cdot 5} = 6\sqrt{5}$$

The geometric mean is significant when the altitude is drawn to the hypotenuse of a right triangle.
The length of the altitude is the geometric mean between each segment of the hypotenuse
> *and*

Each leg is the geometric mean between the hypotenuse and the segment of the hypotenuse that is adjacent to the leg.

Example:

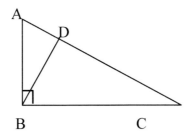

$\triangle$ABC is a right $\triangle$
$\angle$ABC is a right $\angle$
AB = 6
AC = 12
Find AD, CD, BD, and BC

$$\frac{12}{6} = \frac{6}{AD}$$

$$\frac{3}{BD} = \frac{BD}{9}$$

$$\frac{12}{BC} = \frac{BC}{9}$$

12(AD) = 36

$(BD)^2 = 27$

$(BC)^2 = 108$

AD = 3

$BD = \sqrt{27} = \sqrt{9 \cdot 3} = 3\sqrt{3}$

$BC = \sqrt{108} = \sqrt{36 \cdot 3} = 6\sqrt{3}$

CD = 12 - 3 = 9

Math Middle School   114

29.3   PYTHAGOREAN THEOREM

The **Pythagorean Theorem** states that in a right triangle, the square of the hypotenuse equals the sum of the squares of the legs. This is commonly written $c^2 = a^2 + b^2$ where c is the hypotenuse and a and b are the legs

<u>Example:</u>

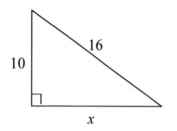

Find the length of the missing side.

$$c^2 = a^2 + b^2$$
$$16^2 = 10^2 + x^2$$
$$256 = 100 + x^2$$
$$x^2 = 156$$
$$x = \sqrt{156} = \sqrt{4 \cdot 39} = 2\sqrt{39}$$

29.4 CONVERSE OF THE PYTHAGOREAN THEOREM

The Converse of the Pythagorean Theorem states that if the square of one side of a triangle is equal to the sum of the squares of the other two sides, then the triangle is a right triangle.

Example:
Given $\triangle XYZ$, with sides measuring 12, 16 and 20 cm. Is this a right triangle?

$$c^2 = a^2 + b^2$$
$$20^2 \ \underline{?} \ 12^2 + 16^2$$
$$400 \ \underline{?} \ 144 + 256$$
$$400 = 400$$

Yes, the triangle is a right triangle.

This theorem can be expanded to determine if triangles are obtuse or acute.

If the square of the longest side of a triangle is greater than the sum of the squares of the other two sides, then the triangle is an obtuse triangle.
and
If the square of the longest side of a triangle is less than the sum of the squares of the other two sides, then the triangle is an acute triangle.

Example:
Given $\triangle LMN$ with sides measuring 7, 12, and 14 inches. Is the triangle right, acute, or obtuse?

$$14^2 \ \underline{?} \ 7^2 + 12^2$$
$$196 \ \underline{?} \ 49 + 144$$
$$196 > 193$$

Therefore, the triangle is obtuse.

29.5   30-60-90 and 45-45-90 RIGHT TRIANGLES

An isosceles right triangle is also called a 45-45-90 right triangle because of the measures of its angles. In a 45-45-90 triangle, the hypotenuse is $\sqrt{2}$ times the length of the leg.

Another special right triangle has angles measuring 30° and 60°. This is called a 30-60-90 right triangle. In a 30-60-90 triangle, the hypotenuse is two times the shorter leg and the longer leg is $\sqrt{3}$ times the length of the shorter leg.

<u>Example 1</u>:

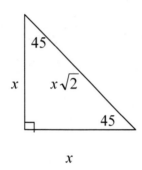

<u>Example 2</u>:

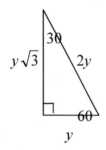

<u>Example 2</u>:

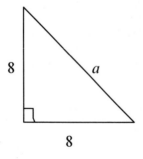

Find *a*. Since this is a right isosceles right triangle, it is also 45-45-90 and the hypotenuse equals $\sqrt{2}$ times the leg. Thus $a = 8\sqrt{2}$.

Example 4:

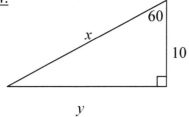

Find the lengths of the missing sides.

Since this is a 30-60-90 right triangle, the hypotenuse is twice the shorter side; thus $x = 20$ and the longer leg is $\sqrt{3}$ times the shorter leg, thus $y = 10\sqrt{3}$.

29.6 and 29.7 TRIGONOMETRY OF RIGHT ANGLES

In the right triangle, the legs can be labeled in relation to a selected angle, as opposite or adjacent.

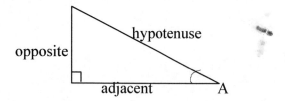

The trigonometric ratios state:

The **tangent** of an angle in a right triangle is the ratio of the leg opposite that angle to the leg adjacent to the angle.

The **sine** of an angle in a right triangle is the ratio of the leg opposite that angle to the hypotenuse.

The **cosine** of an angle in a right triangle is the ratio of the leg adjacent to that angle to the hypotenuse.

Simply,

$$\tan = \frac{opp}{adj}$$

$$\sin = \frac{opp}{hyp}$$

$$\cos = \frac{adj}{hyp}$$

By using the table of trigonometric ratios, the measures of sides and angles of right triangles can be calculated. Since the values in the chart are approximate, rounded to four decimal places, we use the symbol "≈" meaning "is approximately equal to."

<u>Example 1</u>: Find the missing side or angle.

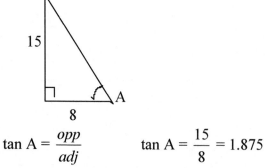

$$\tan A = \frac{opp}{adj} \qquad \tan A = \frac{15}{8} = 1.875$$

Looking on the trigonometric chart, the angle whose tangent is closest to 1.875 is 62°.
Thus ∠A ≈ 62°

Example 2:

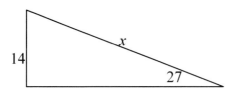

$$\sin A = \frac{opp}{hyp}$$

$$\sin 27^{\circ} = \frac{14}{x}$$

$$0.4540 \approx \frac{14}{x}$$

$$x \approx \frac{14}{.454}$$

$$x \approx 30.8$$

Example 3:

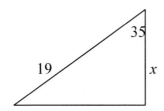

$$\cos A = \frac{adj}{hyp}$$

$$\cos 35^{\circ} = \frac{x}{19}$$

$$x \approx 19 \times .819$$

$$x \approx 15.56$$

30. CIRCLES

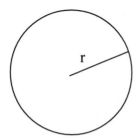 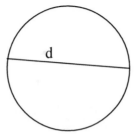 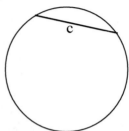

A line segment drawn from the center of a circle to any point on the circle is a **radius.** A line segment drawn from any point on a circle to another point on the circle, passing through the center of the circle is a **diameter.** A **chord** is a segment drawn from a point on the circle to any point on the circle.

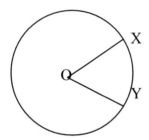

A **central angle** is the angle formed by two radii intersecting in the center of a circle. The parts of a circle determined by the endpoints of the radii on the circles are arcs. The minor arc is formed by the acute angle and the major arc is determined by the reflexive angle.

Example:
If $\angle XOY = 40°$, find the measure of major arc XY and minor arc XY.

The measure of minor arc XY also equals $40°$. The major arc measures $360 - 40 = 320°$.

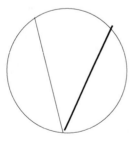

An **inscribed angle** is an angle formed by the intersection of two chords. The measure of an inscribed angle is equal to one-half the measure of the intercepted arc.

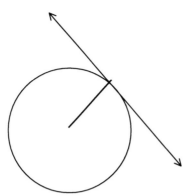

A **tangent** to a circle is a line intersecting that circle at exactly one point. A radius drawn to the point of intersection will always be perpendicular to the tangent.

31. BASIC CONSTRUCTIONS

Bisecting angles and segments, constructing segments, angles, perpendiculars, parallels, tangents and circles

See Geometry references

32. AXIOMATIC APPROACH TO PROOFS FOR THEOREMS

A logical statement may be written in the **conditional** form,
　　　If p, then q
where p is the hypothesis and q is the conclusion.

The **converse** is
　　　If q, then p

Two statements are converses of each other when the hypothesis of one is the conclusion of the other.

Example:
Statement:　If $ab = 0$, then $a = 0$ or $b = 0$
Converse:　If $a = 0$ or $b = 0$, then $ab = 0$

The **inverse** is
　　　If not p, then not q
and the **contrapositive** is
　　　If not q, then not p

A statement and its contrapositive are logically equivalent. Therefore if a statement is true it follows that its contrapositive will also be true.

Example:
Statement:　All squares are rectangles.
　　　That is, if a quadrilateral is a square, then it is a rectangle.
Contrapositive:　If a quadrilateral is not a rectangle, then it is not a square.

33. PROBLEM SOLVING AND GEOMETRIC PROOFS

33.1 CONGRUENT TRIANGLES

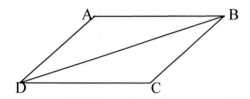

Given: Parallelogram ABCD
Prove: $\triangle ABD \cong \triangle BCD$

1. ABCD is a parallelogram	Given
2. AB $\cong$ CD and AD $\cong$ BC	Opposite sides of a parallelogram are congruent
3. BD $\cong$ BD	Reflexive
4. $\triangle$ ABD $\cong$ $\triangle$BCD	SSS

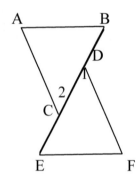

Given: AB $\|$ EF, DF $\|$ AC
       BD $\cong$ CE
Prove: $\triangle ABC \cong \triangle DEF$

1. AB $\|$ EF, DF $\|$ AC BD $\cong$ CE	Given
2. CD $\cong$ CD	Reflexive
3. BC $\cong$ DE	Addition
4. $\angle 1 \cong \angle 2$	If two lines are parallel, then their alternate interior angles are congruent.
5. $\angle B \cong \angle F$	If two lines are parallel, then their alternate interior angles are congruent.
6. $\triangle ABC \cong \triangle DEF$	ASA

33.2 RIGHT TRIANGLES

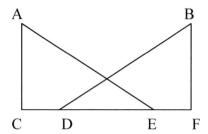

Given: AC $\perp$ CF and BF $\perp$ CF
       CD $\cong$ EF and AE $\cong$ BD
Prove: $\triangle$ ACE $\cong$ $\triangle$BDF

1. AC $\perp$ CF and BF $\perp$ CF   Given
   CD $\cong$ EF and AE $\cong$ BD
2. DE $\cong$ DE   Reflexive
3. CE $\cong$ DF   Addition
4. $\angle$ACF is a right angle   Perpendicular lines form right angles
    $\angle$BFC is a right angle
5. $\triangle$ACE and $\triangle$BDF are right triangles   A right triangle has a right angle.
6. $\triangle$ACE $\cong$ $\triangle$BDF   HL

33.3 OVERLAPPING TRIANGLES

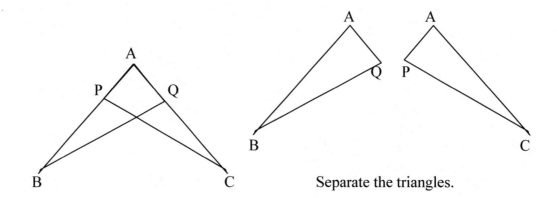

Separate the triangles.

Given: PC⊥AB and BQ⊥AC
        AP ≅ AQ
Prove: △ACP ≅ △ABQ

1. PC⊥AB and BQ⊥AC AP ≅ AQ	Given
2. ∠A ≅ ∠A	Reflexive
3. ∠AQB and ∠APC are right ∠s	Perpendicular lines intersect to form right angles
4. ∠AQB ≅ ∠APC	All right angles are congruent
5. △ACP ≅ △ABQ	ASA

33.4   PARALLELOGRAMS

A parallelogram is a quadrilateral with both pairs of opposite sides parallel.

Theorems:

1. Consecutive pairs of angles are supplementary.
2. Opposite angles are congruent.
3. A diagonal divides the parallelogram into two congruent triangles.
4. Opposite sides are congruent
5. Diagonals bisect each other.

Example:

Given: Parallelogram ABCD,
with diagonals AC and BD
intersecting at E
Prove: $AE \cong DE$

1. Parallelogram ABCD, with diagonals AC and BD intersecting at E	Given
2. AB $\parallel$ CD	Opposite sides of a parallelogram are parallel
3. $\angle BCD \cong \angle ABC$	If parallel lines are cut by a transversal, their alternate interior angles are congruent.
4. AB $\cong$ CD	Opposite sides of a parallelogram are congruent.
5. $\angle BAD \cong \angle ADC$	If parallel lines are cut by a transversal, their alternate interior angles are congruent.
6. $\triangle ABE \cong \triangle CDE$	ASA
7. $AE \cong DE$	Corresponding parts of congruent triangles are congruent.

33.5   PROVING A QUADRILATERAL IS A PARALLELOGRAM

A quadrilateral is a parallelogram if any <u>one</u> of these are true:

1. One pair of opposite sides is both parallel and congruent.
2. Both pairs of opposite sides are congruent.
3. Both pairs of opposite angles are congruent.
4. The diagonals bisect each other.

<u>Example:</u>

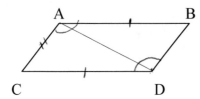

Given: Quadrilateral ABCD
$\qquad$ AB $\cong$ CD
$\qquad$ $\angle$BAC $\cong$ $\angle$CDB
Prove: ABCD is a parallelogram.

1. Quadrilateral ABCD $\quad$ AB $\cong$ CD $\quad$ $\angle$BAC $\cong$ $\angle$CDB	Given
2. AC $\cong$ AC	Reflexive
3. $\triangle$ABD $\cong$ $\triangle$ACD	SAS
4. AD $\cong$ BC	Corresponding parts of congruent triangles are congruent.
5. ABCD is a parallelogram	If both pairs of opposite sides of a quadrilateral are congruent, the quadrilateral is a parallelogram.

33.6   RECTANGLES, RHOMBUSES AND SQUARES

A **rectangle** is a parallelogram with a right angle.

Rectangles have all the properties of parallelograms.
In addition, all four angles are right angles and
the diagonals are congruent.

A **rhombus** is a parallelogram with all sides equal length.

Rhombuses have all the properties of parallelograms.
In addition, a rhombus is equilateral,
     the diagonals are perpendicular and
     the diagonals bisect the angles.

A **square** is a rectangle with all sides equal length.

Squares have all the properties of rectangles and
all the properties of rhombuses.

33.7   TRAPEZOIDS

A **trapezoid** is a quadrilateral with <u>exactly</u> one pair of opposite sides parallel. The parallel sides are called bases; the non-parallel sides are legs. In an **isosceles trapezoid,** the legs are congruent.

An **altitude** is a line segment drawn from a point on either base, perpendicular to the opposite base. The **median** is a line segment that joins the midpoints of each leg.

Theorems:

1. The median of a trapezoid is parallel to the bases and equal to one-half the sum of the lengths of the bases.

2. The base angles of an isosceles trapezoid are congruent.

3. The diagonals of an isosceles trapezoid are congruent.

<u>Example</u>:

In trapezoid ABCD, AB = 17 and CD = 21. Find the length of the median.
The median is one-half the sum of the bases.
$\frac{1}{2}(17 + 21) = 19$

33.8   MIDPOINTS OF A TRIANGLE

Theorem: The line segment joining the midpoints of two sides of a triangle is parallel to the third side and equal to one-half its length.

Example:

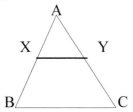

In triangle ABC, X is the midpoint of side AB and Y is the midpoint of side AC. If BC = 22m, find the length of XY.

$XY = \frac{1}{2}(BC) = \frac{1}{2}(22) = 11$

33.9   BISECTORS

A **bisector of an angle** is a ray that divides the angle into two congruent angles. Any angle has exactly one bisector.

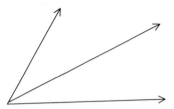

Any point on the bisector of an angle is equidistant from both rays forming that angle. Conversely, if a point is equidistant from the rays forming an angle, that point determines the bisector of that angle.

The **bisector of a line segment** is any line that intersects the line segment at its midpoint. A line segment has exactly one bisector.

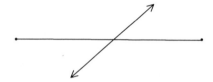

A line cannot be bisected since it extends endlessly in both directions.

The **perpendicular bisector** of a segment is a line that is both perpendicular to and bisects the line segment.

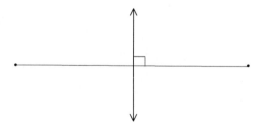

The distance from a point to a line is the length of the perpendicular from that point to the line.
Any point on the perpendicular bisector of a line segment is equidistant from the ends of the segment.
Conversely, if two points are equidistant from the ends of a line segment, the points determine the perpendicular bisector of the segment.

33.10 MEDIAN and ALTITUDE OF A TRIANGLE

A **median** of a triangle is a line segment drawn from a vertex to the midpoint of the opposite side.

An **altitude** of a triangle is a line segment drawn from a vertex perpendicular to the opposite side.

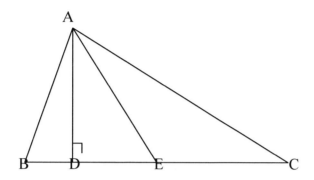

In $\triangle ABC$, $AD \perp BC$ and $BE \cong CE$. therefore, AD is an altitude and AE is a median.

Example:

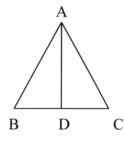

Given: $\triangle ABC$ with
         altitude CD and median CD
Prove: $\triangle ADB \cong \triangle ACD$

1. CD is an altitude CD is a median	Given
2. AD $\perp$ BC	Definition of altitude
3. $\angle ADB$ and $\angle ADC$ are right angles.	Perpendicular lines form right angles.
4. $\angle ADB \cong \angle ADC$	All right angles are congruent.
5. BD $\cong$ CD	Definition of median
6. AD $\cong$ AD	Reflexive
7. $\triangle ADB \cong \triangle ACD$	SAS

33.11 BISECTOR OF AN ANGLE OF A TRIANGLE

The **angle bisector** of a triangle is a line segment that bisects any angle and ends in the side opposite that angle.

If the angle bisector of a triangle is perpendicular to the base, it bisects the base.
The bisector of the vertex angle of an isosceles triangle bisects the base.

Theorem: The angle bisector of a triangle forms two line segments that are proportional to their adjacent sides.

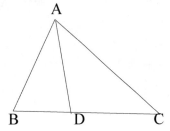

In $\triangle$ ABC, AD bisects $\angle$BAC. The following proportion is true about the lengths of the line segments. $\dfrac{BD}{AB} = \dfrac{CD}{AC}$

33.12 ADDITIONAL THEOREMS

The intersection of two parallel planes and a third plane is two parallel lines .

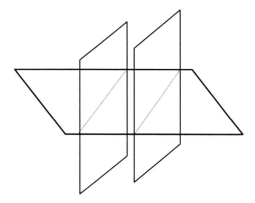

Exactly one line can be drawn parallel to a given line through a point outside that line.

Exactly one line can be drawn perpendicular to a given line through a point outside that line.

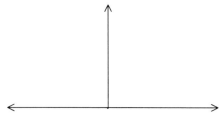

34. PROBLEM SOLVING USING COORDINATE GEOMETRY

34.1   DISTANCE FORMULA

The distance formula is used to find the distance between two points on the coordinate plane, or the length of the line connecting those points.

The distance PQ between points $P(x_1 \; y_2)$ and $Q(x_1 \; y_2)$ is

$$PQ = \sqrt{(x_1 - x_2)^2 + (y_1 - y_2)^2}$$

Example: Find the length of line segment AB for A(-3, 8) and B(4, -2).

$$AB = \sqrt{(-3 - 4)^2 + (8 - {}^-2)^2}$$

$$\sqrt{(-7)^2 + 10^2}$$

$$\sqrt{49 + 100}$$

$$\sqrt{149}$$

$$\approx 12$$

34.2   EQUATION OF A CIRCLE

The **equation of a circle with center (0,0) and radius r** is
$$x^2 + y^2 = r^2$$

Example:
Write the equation of a circle with center (0,0) and radius 6.
$$x^2 + y^2 = 36$$

The **equation of a circle with center (a,b) and radius r** is

$$(x - a)^2 + (y - b)^2 = r^2$$

Example 1:
Write the equation of circle with center (3, -7) and radius 5.
$$(x - 3)^2 + (y + 7)^2 = 25$$

Example 2:
Find the radius and coordinates of the center of a circle with the equation
$$(x - 4)^2 + (y + 2)^2 = 18$$

center is (4, -2)   radius = $\sqrt{18}$ = $3\sqrt{2}$

35   CURRICULUM AND INSTRUCTION

The National Council of Teachers of Mathematics standards emphasize the teacher's obligation to make mathematics relevant to the students and applicable to the real world. The mathematics need in our technological society is different from that need in the past; we need thinking skills rather than computational. Mathematics needs to connect to other subjects, as well as other areas of math.

ERROR ANALYSIS

A simple method for analyzing student errors is to ask how the answer was obtained. The teacher can then determine if a common error pattern has resulted in the wrong answer. There is a value to having the students explain how the arrived at the correct as well as the incorrect answers.

Many errors are due to simple **carelessness**. Students need to be encouraged to work slowly and carefully. They should check their calculations by redoing the problem on another paper, not merely looking at the work. Addition and subtraction problems need to be written neatly so the numbers line up. Students need to be careful regrouping in subtraction. Students must write clearly and legibly, including erasing fully. Use estimation to ensure that answers make sense.

Many students computational skills exceed their **reading** level. Although they can understand basic operations, they fail to grasp the concept or completely understand the question. Students must read directions slowly.

Fractions are often a source of many errors. Students need to be reminded to use common denominators when adding and subtracting and to always express answers in simplest terms. Again, it is helpful to check by estimating.

The most common error that is made when working with **decimals** is failure to line up the decimal points when adding or subtracting or not moving the decimal point when multiplying or dividing. Students also need to be reminded to add zeroes when necessary. Reading aloud may also be beneficial. Estimation, as always, is especially important.

Students need to know that it is okay to make mistakes. The teacher must keep a positive attitude, so they do not feel defeated or frustrated.

REPRESENTATIONS OF CONCEPTS

Mathematical operations can be shown using manipulatives or drawings.
Multiplication can be shown using arrays.

3×4
□ □ □ □
□ □ □ □
□ □ □ □

Addition and subtractions can be demonstrated with symbols.

ψ ψ ψ ξ ξ ξ
$3 + 4 = 7$
$7 - 3 = 4$

Fractions can be clarified using pattern blocks, fraction bars, or paper folding.

CONCEPT DEVELOPMENT

Manipulatives can foster learning for all students. Mathematics needs to be derived from something that is real to the learner. If he can "touch" it, he will understand and remember. Students can use fingers, ice cream sticks, tiles and paper folding, as well as those commercially available manipulatives to visualize operations and concepts. The teacher needs to solidify the concrete examples into abstract mathematics.

PROBLEM SOLVING

Problem solving strategies are simply plans of attack. Student often panic when confronted with word problems. If they have a "list" of ideas, ways to attempt a solution, they will be able to approach the problems more calmly and confidently. Some methods include, but are not limited to, draw a diagram, work backwards, guess and check, and solve a simpler problem.

It is helpful to have students work in groups. Mathematics does not have to be solitary activity. Cooperative learning fosters enthusiasm. Creating their own problems is another useful tool. Also, encourage students to find more than one way to solve a problem. Thinking about problem solving after the solution has been discovered encourages understanding and creativity. The more they practice problems, the more comfortable and positive students will feel.

MATHEMATICAL LANGUAGE

Students need to use the proper mathematical terms and expressions. When reading decimals, they need to read 0.4 as "four tenths" to promote better understanding of the concepts. They should do their work in a neat and organized manner. Students need to be encouraged to verbalize their strategies, both in computation and word problems. Additionally, writing original word problems fosters understanding of math language. Another idea is requiring students to develop their own glossary of mathematical glossary. Knowing the answers and being able to communicate them are equally important.

MANIPULATIVES

Example:
Using tiles to demonstrate both geometric ideas and number theory.

Give each group of students 12 tiles and instruct them to build rectangles. Students draw their rectangles on paper.

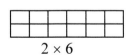

12×1

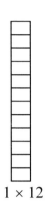

1×12

3×4

4×3

6×2

2×6

Encourage students to describe their reactions. Extend to 16 tiles. Ask students to form additional problems.

CALCULATORS

Calculators are an important tool. They should be encouraged in the classroom and at home. They do not replace basic knowledge but they can relieve the tedium of mathematical computations, allowing students to explore more challenging mathematical directions. Students will be able to use calculators more intelligently if they are taught how. Students need to always check their work by estimating. The goal of mathematics is to prepare the child to survive in the real world. Technology is a reality in today's society.

CHILD DEVELOPMENT

Means of instruction need to be varied to reach children of different skilll levels and learning styles. In addition to directed instruction, students should work cooperatively, explore hands-on activities and do projects.

COMPUTERS

Computers can not replace teachers. However, they can be used to enhance the curriculum. They may be used cautiously to help students practice basic skills. Many excellent programs exist to encourage higher-order thinking skills, creativity and problem solving. Learning to use technology appropriately is an important preparation for adulthood. Computers can also show the connections between mathematics and the real world.

QUESTIONING TECHNIQUES

As the teacher's role in the classroom changes from lecturer to facilitator, the questions need to further stimulate students in various ways.

- Helping students work together

What do you think about what John said?

Do you agree? Disagree?

Can anyone explain that differently?

- Helping students determine for themselves if an answer is correct

What do you think that is true?

How did you get that answer?

Do you think that is reasonable? Why?

- Helping students learn to reason mathematically

Will that method always work?

Can you think of a case where it is not true?

How can you prove that?

Is that answer true in all cases?

- Helping student brainstorm and problem solve

Is there a pattern?

What else can you do?

Can you predict the answer?

What if...?

- Helping students connect mathematical ideas

What did we learn before that is like this?

Can you give an example?

What math did you see on television last night? in the newspaper?

Sources for Review

Bendick, Jeanne (1989). *Mathematics Illustrated Dictionary.* New York: Franklin Watts.

Bennett, A. B., Jr., & Nelson, L. T. (1985). *Mathematics: An informal approach.* (2nd ed.)Boston: Allyn and Bacon.

Bittinger, M. L. & Crown, J. C. (1989). *Mathematics and Calculus with Applications.* Reading, MA: Addison-Wesley Publishing Company.

Cohen, M. P., Elgarten, G. H., Gardella, F. J., Lewis, W. S., Meldon, J. E., & Weingarden, M. S. (1992). *Essentials for High School Mathematics* (teacher's ed.). Boston: Houghton Mifflin Company.

Coxford, A.F. & Payne, J. N. (1983). *HBJ Algebra 2 with Trigonometry.* (teacher's ed.). Orlando, FL: Harcourt, Brace Jovanovich, Inc.

Daintith, J., & Nelson, R. D. (1989). *The Penguin Dictionary of Mathematics.* London: Penguin Books.

Davidson, P. (1984). *Everyday Math Made Easy.* New York: McGraw-Hill.

Dolciani, M. P., Wooton, W., Beckenbach, E.F., & Sharron, S. (1974) *Algebra 2 and Trigonometry.* (teacher's ed.). Boston: Houghton, Mifflin Company.

Dressler, I., Keenan, E. P., Gantert, A.X., Occhiogrosso, M. (1989). *Integrated Mathematics: Course I* (2nd ed.). New York: Amsco School Publications.

Erdsneker, B. (1982). *Mathematics Simplified and Self-Taught.* New York: Prentice Hall.

Frederick, M. M., Leinwand, S.J., Postman, R. D., & Wantuck, L. R. (1993). *Practical Mathematics: Skills and Concepts* (teacher's ed.). New York: Holt, Rinehart and Winston.

Frieder, D. (1987), *Clear & Simple Geometry.* New York: Simon & Schuster.

Geltner, P. B., & Peterson, D. J. (1991). *Geometry for College Students.* (2nd ed.). Boston: PWS-Kent Publishing Company.

Harcourt Brace Jovanovich, Inc. (1992). *Mathematics Plus 7.* (Teacher's Ed.). Orlando: Author.

Hirsch, C. R., Roberts, M. A., Coblentz, D. O., Samide, A. J., Schoen, H. (1979). *Geometry*. (teacher's ed.). Glenview, IL: Scott, Foresman and Company.

Jurgensen, R.C., Brown, R.G., Jurgensen, J.W. (1985). *Geometry*. Boston: Houghton Mifflin Company

Keenan, E. P. & Dressler, I. (1981). *Integrated Mathematics: Course II*. New York: Amsco School Publications.

Keenan, E. P. & Gantert, A. X. (1982). *Integrated Mathematics: Course III*. New York: Amsco School Publications.

Larson, R. E. & Hostetler, R. P. (1989). *Precalculus*. Lexington, MA: D. C. Heath and Company.

Lassiter, K. (1993). *Math Matters for Adults: Measurement, Geometry and Algebra*. Texas: Steck-Vaughn.

Leff, L. S. (1990). *Geometry the Easy Way*. New York: Barron's Educational Services.

Leff, L. S. (1988). *Let's Review: Sequential Mathematics, Course I*. New York: Barron's Educational Services.

McConnell, J. W., Brown, S., Eddins, S., Hackworth, M., Sachs, L., Woodward, E., Flanders, J., Hirschhorn, D., Hynes, C., Polonsky, L., & Usiskin, Z. (1990). *USCMP Algebra*. Glenview, IL: Scott, Foresman and Company.

Miller, C. D., Heeren, V. H., & Hornsby, E. J., Jr. (1990). *Mathematical ideas* (6th ed.) Glenview, IL: Scott, Foresman and Company.

Mitchell, R. & Prickel, D. (1984). *Number Power: The real world of adult math: Geometry*. Chicago: Contemporary Books, Inc.

Mitchell, R. (1988). *Number Power: The real world of adult math: Algebra*. Chicago: Contemporary Books, Inc.

National Council of Teachers of Mathematics. (1991). *Professional Standards for Teaching Mathematics*. Reston, VA: Author.

National Council of Teachers of Mathematics. (1964). *Topics in Mathematics for Elementary School Teachers: Twenty-ninth yearbook*. Reston, VA: Author.

National Council of Teachers of Mathematics. (1969). *More Topics in Mathematics for Elementary School Teachers: Thirtieth yearbook*. Washington, DC: Author.

National Council of Teachers of Mathematics. (1970). *The Teaching of Secondary School Mathematics*: *Thirty-third yearbook*. Reston, VA: Author.

Pascoe, L. C. (1992). *Teach Yourself Mathematics.* Chicago: NTC Publishing Group.

Rich, B. (1985). *Mathematics for the College Boards.* New York: Amsco School Publications, Inc.

Schoen, H. L. & Zweng, M. J. (1986) *Estimation and Mental Computation.* Reston, VA: National Council of Teachers of Mathematics.

Sobel, M. A., Maletsky, E.M., Lerner, N., & Cohen, L.S. (1985). *Algebra I.* New York: Harper & Row

Swokowski, E. W. & Cole, J. A. (1993). *Fundamentals of Algebra & Trigonometry* (8th ed.). Boston: PWS Publishing Co.

Thompson, D. R. & Van Loy, M. (1987). *Fundamental Skills of Mathematics.* Clearwater, FL: H & H Publishing Company.

Tobias, S. (1978). *Overcoming Math Anxiety.* New York: W. W. Norton & Company.

Trafton, P.R. & Shulte, A.P. (1989). *New Directions for Elementary School Mathematics: 1989 Yearbook.* Reston,VA: National Council of Teachers of Mathematics.

Usiskin, Z., Flanders, J., Hynes, C., Polonsky, L., Porter, S., & Viktora, S. (1990). *UCSMP Transition Mathematics.* Glenview, IL: Scott, Foresman and Company.

Willoughby, S.S. (1990). *Mathematics Education for a Changing World.* Alexandria, VA: Association for Supervision and Curriculum development.

PRACTICE EXAM   MATHEMATICS MIDDLE SCHOOL

COMPETENCY 1

1) Given W = whole numbers
   N = natural numbers
   Z = integers
   R = rational numbers
   I = irrational numbers

   Which of the following is not true?

   A) $R \subset I$

   B) $W \subset Z$

   C) $Z \subset R$

   D) $N \subset W$

2) **Which of the following is an irrational number?**

   A) .362626262...

   B) $4\frac{1}{3}$

   C) $\sqrt{5}$

   D) $-\sqrt{16}$

3) **Which denotes a complex number?**

   A) 4.1212121212...

   B) $-\sqrt{16}$

   C) $\sqrt{127}$

   D) $\sqrt{-100}$

4) **Choose the correct statement:**

   A)   Rational and irrational numbers are both proper subsets of the real numbers.

   B) The set of whole numbers is a proper subset of the set of natural numbers.

   C) The set of integers is a proper subset of the set of irrational numbers.

   D) The set of real numbers is a proper subset of the natural, whole, integers, rational, and irrational numbers.

COMPETENCY 2

5) **Which statement is an example of the identity axiom of addition?**

   A) 3 + -3 = 0

   B) 3x = 3x + 0

   C) $3 \square \frac{1}{3} = 1$

   D) 3 + 2x = 2x + 3

6) Which axiom is incorrectly applied?

$$3x + 4 = 7$$

Step a $3x + 4 - 4 = 7 - 4$

additive equality

Step b $3x + 4 - 4 = 3$

commutative axiom of addition

Step c. $3x + 0 = 3$

additive inverse

Step d. $3x = 3$

additive identity

A) step a

B) step b

C) step c

D) step d

7) Which of the following sets is closed under division?

A) integers

B) rational numbers

C) natural numbers

D) whole numbers

8) How many real numbers lie between -1 and +I ?

A) 0

B) 1

C) 17

D) an infinite number

COMPETENCY 3

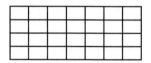

9) The above diagram would be least appropriate for illustrating which of the following?

A) $7 \times 4 + 3$

B) $31 \div 8$

C) 28×3

D) $31 - 3$

10) $24 - 3 \times 7 + 2 =$

A) 5

B) 149

C) −3

D) 189

11) Which of the following does not correctly relate an inverse operation?

A) $a - b = a + -b$

B) $a \times b = b \div a$

C) $\sqrt{a^2} = a$

D) $a \times \dfrac{1}{a} = 1$

12) Mr. Brown feeds his cat premium cat food which costs $40 per month. Approximately how much will it cost to feed her for one year?

A) $500

B) $400

C) $80

D) $4800

COMPETENCY 4

13) Given that n is a positive even integer, 5n + 4 will always be divisible by:

A)   4

B)   5

C)   5n

D)   2

14) Given that x, y, and z are prime numbers, which of the following is true?

A) x + y is always prime

B) xyz is always prime

C) xy is sometimes prime

D) x + y is sometimes prime

15) Find the GCF of $2^2 \cdot 3^2 \cdot 5$ and $2^2 \cdot 3 \cdot 7$.

A) $2^5 \cdot 3^3 \cdot 5 \cdot 7$

B) $2 \cdot 3 \cdot 5 \cdot 7$

C) $2^2 \cdot 3$

D) $2^3 \cdot 3^2 \cdot 5 \cdot 7$

16) Given even numbers x and y, which could be the LCM of x and y?

A) $\dfrac{xy}{2}$

B) 2xy

C) 4xy

D) xy

COMPETENCY 5

17) $(3.8 \times 10^{17}) \times (.5 \times 10^{-12})$

   A) 19×10^5

   B) 1.9×10^5

   C) 1.9×10^6

   D) 1.9×10^7

18) 2^{-3} is equivalent to

   A) .8

   B) -.8

   C) 125

   D) 0.125

19) $\dfrac{3.5 \times 10^{-10}}{0.7 \times 10^4}$

   A) 0.5×10^6

   B) 5.0×10^{-6}

   C) 5.0×10^{-14}

   D) 0.5×10^{-14}

COMPETENCY 6

20) Solve for x: $\dfrac{4}{x} = \dfrac{8}{3}$

   A) .66666...

   B) .6

   C) 15

   D) 1.5

21) Choose the set in which the members are <u>not</u> equivalent.

   A) 1/2 , 0.5 , 50%

   B) 10/5 , 2.0 , 200%

   C) 3/8 , 0.385, 38.5%

   D) 7/10 , 0.7 , 70%

22) If three cups of concentrate are needed to make 2 gallons of fruit punch, how many cups are needed to make 5 gallons?

   A) 6 cups

   B) 7 cups

   C) 7.5 cups

   D) 10 cups

23) A sofa sells for $520. If the retailer makes a 30% profit, what was the wholesale price?

 A) $400

 B) $676

 C) $490

 D) $364

COMPETENCY 7

24) Given a spinner with the numbers one through eight, what is the probability that you will spin an even number or a number greater than four?

 A) 1/4

 B) 1/2

 C) 3/4

 D) 1

25) If a horse will probably win three races out of ten, what are the odds that he will win?

 A) 3:10

 B) 7:10

 C) 3:7

 D) 7:3

26) Given a drawer with 5 black socks, 3 blue socks, and 2 red socks, what is the probability that you will draw two black socks in two draws in a dark room?

 A) 2/9

 B) 1/4

 C) 17/18

 D) 1/18

27) A sack of candy has 3 peppermints, 2 butterscotch drops and 3 cinnamon drops. One candy is drawn and replaced, then another candy is drawn; what is the probability that both will be butterscotch?

 A) 1/2

 B) 1/28

 C) 1/4

 D) 1/16

COMPETENCY 8

28) Find the median of the following set of data:
14 3 7 6 11 20

A) 9

B) 8.5

C) 7

D) 11

29) Corporate salaries are listed for several employees. Which would be the best measure of central tendency?

$24,000 $24,000 $26,000
$28,000 $30,000 $120,000

A) mean

B.) median

C) mode

D) no difference

30) Which statement is true about George's budget?

A) George spends the greatest portion of his income on food.

B) George spends twice as much on utilities as he does on his utilities mortgage.

C) George spends twice as much on utilities as he does on food.

D) George spends the same amount on food and utilities as he does on mortgage.

31) A student scored in the 87th percentile on a standardized test. Which would be the best interpretation of his score?

A) Only 13% of the students who took the test scored higher.

B) This student should be getting mostly B's on his report card.

C) This student performed below average on the test.

D) This is the equivalent of missing 13 questions on a 100 question exam.

COMPETENCY 10

32) A man's waist measures 90 cm. What is the greatest possible error for the measurement?

A) $\pm$ 1 m

B) $\pm$ 8 cm

C) $\pm$ 1 cm

D) $\pm$ 5 mm

33) The mass of a cookie is closest to

A) 0.5 kg

B) 0.5 grams

C) 15 grams

D) 1.5 grams

34) 3 km is equivalent to

A) 300 cm

B) 300 m

C) 3000 cm

D) 3000 m

35) 4 square yards is equivalent to

A) 12 square feet

B) 48 square feet

C) 36 square feet

D) 108 square feet

COMPETENCY 11

36) If a circle has an area of 25 cm^2, what is its circumference to the nearest tenth of a centimeter?

A) 78.5 cm

B) 17.7 cm

C) 8.9 cm

D) 15.7 cm

37) Find the area of the figure below.

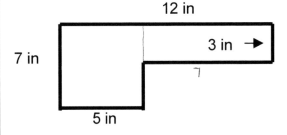

A) 56 in^2

B) 27 in^2

C) 71 in^2

D) 170 in^2

38) Find the area of the shaded region given square ABCD with side AB=10m and circle E.

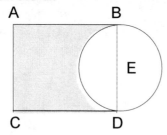

A) 178.5 m^2

B) 139.25 m^2

C) 71 m^2

D) 60.75 m^2

39) Given similar polygons with corresponding sides of lengths 9 and 15, find the perimeter of the smaller polygon if the perimeter of the larger polygon is 150 units.

A) 54

B) 135

C) 90

D) 126

40)

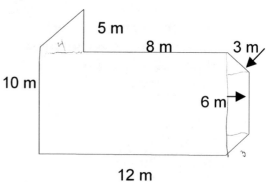

Compute the area of the polygon shown above.

A) 178 m^2

B) 154 m^2

C) 43 m^2

D) 188 m^2

COMPETENCY 12

41) If the radius of a right circular cylinder is doubled, how does its volume change?

A) no change

B) also is doubled

C) four times the original

D) pi times the original

42) Determine the volume of a sphere to the nearest cm if the surface area is 113 cm^2.

    A) 113 cm^3

    B) 339 cm^3

    C) 37.7 cm^3

    D) 226 cm3

43) Compute the surface area of the prism.

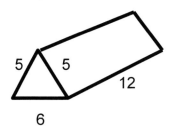

    A) 204

    B) 216

    C) 360

    D) 180

44) If the base of a regular square pyramid is tripled, how does its volume change?

    A) double the original

    B) triple the original

    C) nine times the original

    D) no change

45) How does lateral area differ from total surface area in prisms, pyramids, and cones?

    A) For the lateral area, only use surfaces perpendicular to the base.

    B) They are both the same.

    C) The lateral area does not include the base.

    D) The lateral area is always a factor of pi.

COMPETENCY 13

46) Given XY $\cong$ YZ and $\angle$AYX $\cong$ $\angle$AYZ. Prove $\triangle$AYZ $\cong$ $\triangle$AYX.

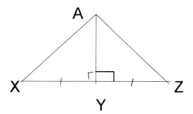

    1) XY $\cong$ YZ

    2) $\angle$AYX $\cong$ $\angle$AYZ

    3) AY $\cong$ AY

    4) $\triangle$AYZ $\cong$ $\triangle$AYX

Which property justifies step 3?

    A) reflexive

    B) symmetric

    C) transitive

    D) identity

47) Given $l_1 \parallel l_2$ prove $\angle b \cong \angle e$

1) $\angle b \cong \angle d$ 1) vertical angle ✓ theorem

2) $\angle d \cong \angle e$ 2) alternate interior angle theorem

3) $\angle b \cong \angle e$ 3) symmetric axiom of equality

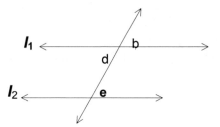

Which step is incorrectly justified?

A) step 1

B) step 2

C) step 3

D) no error

COMPETENCY 14

48) Simplify $\dfrac{\frac{3}{4}x^2y^{-3}}{\frac{2}{3}xy}$

A) $\dfrac{1}{2}xy^{-4}$

B) $\dfrac{1}{2}x^{-1}y^{-4}$

C) $\dfrac{9}{8}xy^{-4}$

D) $\dfrac{9}{8}xy^{-2}$

49) $7t - 4 \cdot 2t + 3t \cdot 4 \div 2 =$

A) $5t$

B) 0

C) $31t$

D) $18t$

COMPETENCY 15

50) Solve for x: $3x + 5 \geq 8 + 7x$

A) $x \geq -\dfrac{3}{4}$

B) $x \leq -\dfrac{3}{4}$

C) $x \geq \dfrac{3}{4}$

D) $x \leq \dfrac{3}{4}$

51) Solve for x: $|2x + 3| > 4$

A) $-\dfrac{7}{2} > x > \dfrac{1}{2}$

B) $-\dfrac{1}{2} > x > \dfrac{7}{2}$

C) $x < \dfrac{7}{2}$ or $x < -\dfrac{1}{2}$

D) $x < -\dfrac{7}{2}$ or $x > \dfrac{1}{2}$

COMPETENCY 16

52) 3x + 2y = 12
    12x + 8y = 15

    A) all real numbers

    B) x = 4, y = 4

    C) x = 2, y = -1

    D) ∅

53) x = 3y + 7
    7x + 5y = 23

    A) (-1,4)

    B) (4, -1)

    C) $(-\frac{29}{7}, -\frac{26}{7})$

    D) (10, 1)

COMPETENCY 17

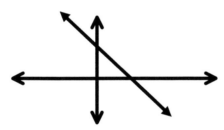

54) Which equation is represented by the above graph?

    A) x - y = 3

    B) x - y = -3

    C) x + y = 3

    D) x + y = -3

55) Graph the solution:
    $|x| + 7 < 13$

    A) (number line, open circles, -6, 0, 6)

    B) (number line, closed circles, -6, 0, 6)

    C) (number line, open circles, -6, 0, 6)

    D) (number line, closed circles, -6, 0, 6)

COMPETENCY 18

56) Three less than four times a number is five times the sum of that number and 6. Which equation could be used to solve this problem?

    A) 3 - 4n = 5(n + 6)

    B) 3 - 4n + 5n = 6

    C) 4n - 3 = 5n + 6

    D) 4n - 3 = 5(n + 6)

57) A boat travels 30 miles upstream in three hours. It makes the return trip in one and a half hours. What is the speed of the boat in still water?

    A) 10 mph

    B) 15 mph

    C) 20 mph

    D) 30 mph

COMPETENCY 19

58) Which set illustrates a function?

A) { (0,1) (0,2) (0,3) (0,4) }

B) { (3,9) (-3,9) (4,16) (-4,16)}

C) { (1,2) (2,3) (3,4) (1,4) }

D) { (2,4) (3,6) (4,8) (4,16) }

59) Give the domain for the function over the set of real numbers:
$$y = \frac{3x + 2}{2x - 3}$$

A) all real numbers

B) all real numbers, $x \neq 0$

C) all real numbers, $x \neq -2$ or 3

D) all real numbers, $x \neq \dfrac{\pm\sqrt{6}}{2}$

COMPETENCY 20

60) Factor completely:
$$8(x - y) + a(y - x)$$

A) $(8 + a)(y - x)$

B) $(8 - a)(y - x)$

C) $(a - 8)(y - x)$

D) $(a - 8)(y + x)$

61) Which of the following is a factor of $k^3 - m^3$?

A) $k^2 + m^2$

B) $k + m$

C) $k^2 - m^2$

D) $k - m$

COMPETENCY 21

62) Solve for x.
$$3x^2 - 2 + 4(x^2 - 3) = 0$$

A) $\{ -\sqrt{2} , \sqrt{2} \}$

B) $\{ 2, -2 \}$

C) $\{ 0, \sqrt{3}, -\sqrt{3} \}$

D) $\{ 7, -7 \}$

63) $\sqrt{75} + \sqrt{147} - \sqrt{48}$

A) 174

B) $12\sqrt{3}$

C) $8\sqrt{3}$

D) 74

COMPETENCY 22

64) The discriminant of a quadratic equation is evaluated and determined to be -3. The equation has

   A) one real root

   B) one complex root

   C) two roots, both real

   D) two roots, both complex

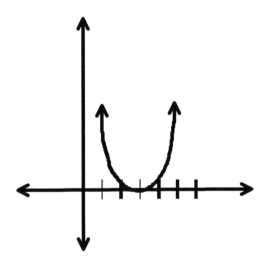

65) Which equation is graphed above?

A) $y = 4 (x + 3)^2$

B) $y = 4 (x - 3)^2$

C) $y = 3 (x - 4)^2$

D) $y = 3 (x + 4)^2$

COMPETENCY 23

66) If y varies inversely as x and x is 4 when y is 6, what is the constant of variation?

   A) 2

   B) 12

   C) 3/2

   D) 24

67) If y varies directly as x and x is 2 when y is 6, what is x when y is 18?

   A) 3

   B) 6

   C) 26

   D) 36

COMPETENCY 24

68) {1,4,7,10, . . .}
What is the 40th term in this sequence?

   A) 43

   B) 121

   C) 118

   D) 120

69) {6,11,16,21, . .}
Find the sum of the first 20
terms in the sequence.

A) 1070

B) 1176

C) 969

D) 1069

COMPETENCY 25

**70) Two non-coplanar lines which
do not intersect are labeled**

A) parallel lines

B) perpendicular lines

C) skew lines

D) alternate exterior lines

71)

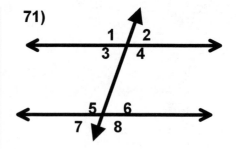

**Given $l_1 \parallel l_2$ which of the
following is true?**

A) $\angle 1$ and $\angle 8$ are congruent
and alternate interior angles

B) $\angle 2$ and $\angle 3$ are congruent
and corresponding angles

C) $\angle 3$ and $\angle 4$ are adjacent and
supplementary angles

D) $\angle 3$ and $\angle 5$ are adjacent and
supplementary angles

COMPETENCY 26

72)

**Given the regular hexagon
above, determine the measure
of angle $\angle 1$.**

A) 30°

B) 60°

C) 120°

D) 45°

73)

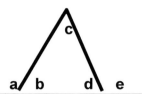

Which of the following statements is true about the number of degrees in each angle?

A) $a + b + c = 180°$

B) $a = e$

C) $b + c = e$

D) $c + d = e$

COMPETENCY 27

74)

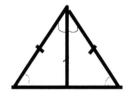

What method could be used to prove the above triangles congruent?

A) SSS

B) SAS

C) AAS

D) SSA

75)

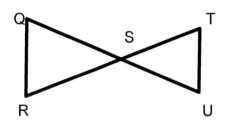

Given **QS ≅ TS and RS ≅US, prove △QRS ≅ △TUS.**

l) QS ≅ TS	1) Given
2) RS ≅ US	2) Given
3) ∠TSU ≅ ∠QSR	3) ?
4) △TSU ≅ △QSR	4) SAS

Give the reason which justifies step 3.

A) Congruent parts of congruent triangles are congruent

B) Reflexive axiom of equality

C) Alternate interior angle Theorem

D) Vertical angle theorem

COMPETENCY 28

76) Given similar polygons with corresponding sides 6 and 8, what is the area of the smaller if the area of the larger is 64?

A) 48

B) 36

C) 144

D) 78

77) In similar polygons, if the perimeters are in a ratio of x:y, the sides are in a ratio of

A) x : y

B) $x^2 : y^2$

C) 2x : y

D) 1/2 x : y

COMPETENCY 29

78)

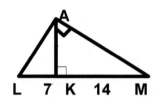

Given altitude AK with measurements as indicated, determine the length of AK.

A) 98

B) $7\sqrt{2}$

C) $\sqrt{21}$

D) $7\sqrt{3}$

79)

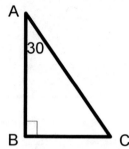

If AC = 12, determine BC.

A) 6

B) 4

C) $6\sqrt{3}$

D) $3\sqrt{6}$

COMPETENCY 30

80)

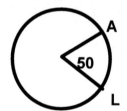

What is the measure of major arc AL ?

A) 50°

B) 25°

C) 100°

D) 310°

81)

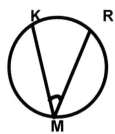

If arc KR = 70° what is the measure of ∠M?

A) 290°

B) 35°

C) 140°

D) 110°

COMPETENCY 31

82)

The above construction can be completed to make

A) an angle bisector

B) parallel lines

C) a perpendicular bisector

D) skew lines

83)

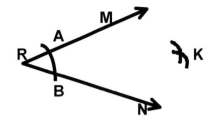

A line from R to K will form

A) an altitude of RMN

B) a perpendicular bisector of MN

C) a bisector of MRN

D) a vertical angle

COMPETENCY 32

84) Which is a postulate?

A) The sum of the angles in any triangle is 180°.

B) A line intersects a plane in one point.

C) Two intersecting lines from congruent vertical angles.

D) Any segment is congruent to itself

85) Which of the following can be defined?

A) point

B) ray

C) line

D) plane

COMPETENCY 33

86)

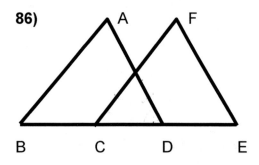

Which theorem could be used to prove △ABD ≅ △CEF, given BC ≅ DE, ∠C ≅ ∠D, and AD ≅ CF?

A) ASA

B) SAS

C) SAA

D) SSS

87)

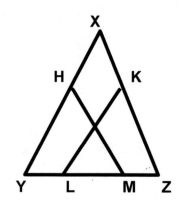

Prove △HYM ≅ △KZL, given XZ ≅ XY and YL ≅ MZ

1) XZ ≅ XY	1) Given
2) ∠Y ≅ ∠Z	2) ?
3) ∠L ≅ ∠M	3) Given
4) YL ≅ MZ	4) Given
5) LM ≅ LM	5) ?
6) YM ≅ LZ	6) Add
7) △HYM ≅ △KZL	7) ASA

Which could be used to justify steps 2 and 5?

A) CPCTC, Identity

B) Isosceles Triangle Theorem, Identity

C) SAS, Reflexive

D) Isosceles Triangle Theorem, Reflexive

COMPETENCY 34

88) **Find the distance between (3,7) and (-3,4).**

    A) 9

    B) 45

    C) $3\sqrt{5}$

    D) $5\sqrt{3}$

89) **Find the midpoint of (2,5) and (7,-4).**

    A) (9,-1)

    B) (5,9)

    C) (9/2 , -1/2)

    D) (9/2, 1/2)

90) **Given segment AC with B as its midpoint find the coordinates of C if A = (5,7) and B = (3, 6.5).**

    A) (4, 6.5)

    B) (1, 6)

    C) (2, 0.5)

    D) (16, 1)

COMPETENCY 35

91)

The above diagram most likely be used in deriving a formula for which of the following?

    A) the area of a rectangle

    B) the area of a triangle

    C) the perimeter of a triangle

    D) the surface area of a prism

92) **A student turns in a paper with this type of error:**

    $7 + 16 \div 8 \times 2 = 8$
    $8 - 3 \times 3 + 4 = -5$

In order to remediate this error, a teacher should:

    A) review and drill basic number facts

    B) emphasize the importance of using parentheses in simplifying expressions

    C) emphasize the importance of working from left to right when applying the order of operations

    D) do nothing; these answers are correct

93) Identify the proper sequencing of subskills when teaching graphing inequalities in two dimensions

   A) shading regions, graphing lines, graphing points, determining whether a line is solid or broken

   B) graphing points, graphing lines, determining whether a line is solid or broken, shading regions

   C) graphing points, shading regions, determining whether a line is solid or broken, graphing lines

   D) graphing lines, determining whether a line is solid or broken, graphing points, shading regions

94) Sandra has $34.00, Carl has $42.00. How much more does Carl have than Sandra?

   Which would be the best method for finding the answer?

   A) addition

   B) subtraction

   C) division

   D) both A and B are equally correct

95) Which is the least appropriate strategy to emphasize when teaching problem solving?

   A) guess and check

   B) look for key words to indicate operations such as all together-add, more than-subtract, times-multiply

   C) make a diagram

   D) solve a simpler version of the problem

96) Choose the least appropriate set of manipulatives for a six grade class.

   A) graphic calculators, compasses, rulers, conic section models

   B) two color counters, origami paper, markers, yarn

   C) balance, meter stick, colored pencils, beads

   D) paper cups, beans, tangrams, geoboards

97) According to Piaget, at which developmental level would a child be able to learn formal algebra?

A) pre-operational

B) sensory-motor

C) abstract

D) concrete operational

98) Which statement is incorrect?

A) Drill and practice is one good use for classroom computers.

B) Some computer programs can help to teach problem solving.

C) Computers are not effective unless each child in the class has his own workstation.

D) Analyzing science project data on a computer during math class is an excellent use of class time.

99) Given a,b,y, and z are real numbers and ay + b = z, Prove

$$y = \frac{z + -b}{a}$$

Statement	Reason
1) ay + b = z	1) Given
2) -b is a real number	2) Closure
3) (ay +b) + -b = z + -b	3) Addition property of Identity
4) ay + (b + -b) = z + -b	4) Associative
5) ay + 0 = z + -b	5) Additive inverse
6) ay = a + -b	6) Addition property of identity
7) a = $\frac{z + -b}{y}$	7) Division

Which reason is incorrect for the corresponding statement?

A) step 3

B) step 4

C) step 5

D) step 6

100) Seventh grade students are working on a project using non-standard measurement. Which would not be an appropriate instrument for measuring the length of the classroom?

A) a student's foot

B) a student's arm span

C) a student's jump

D) all are appropriate

Math Middle School 168

Answer Key Math Middle School

1. A	26. A	51. D	76. B
2. C	27. D	52. D	77. A
3. D	28. A	53. B	78. B
4. A	29. B	54. C	79. A
5. B	30. C	55. A	80. D
6. B	31. A	56. D	81 B
7. B	32. D	57. B	82. C
8. D	33. C	58. B	83. C
9. B	34. D	59. D	84. D
10. A	35. C	60. C	85. B
11. B	36. B	61. D	86. B
12. A	37. A	62. A	87. D
13. D	38. D	63. C	88. C
14. D	39. C	64. D	89. D
15. C	40. B	65. B	90. B
16. A	41. C	66. D	91. B
17. B	42. A	67. B	92. C
18. D	43. B	68. C	93. B
19. C	44. B	69. A	94. D
20. D	45. C	70. C	95. B
21. C	46. A	71. C	96. A
22. C	47. C	72. A	97. C
23. A	48. C	73. C	98. C
24. C	49. A	74. B	99. D
25. C	50. B	75. D	100. D

Explanation of Solutions

The following represent one way to solve the problems and obtain a correct answer.
There are many other mathematically correct ways of determining the correct answer.

1) A   The rational numbers are not a subset of the irrational numbers. All of the other statements are true.

2) C   5 is an irrational number A and B can both be expressed as fractions. D can be simplified to -4, an integer and rational number.

3) D   A complex number is the square root of a negative number. The complex number is defined as the square root of -1. A is rational, B and C are irrational.

4) A   A proper subset is completely contained in but not equal to the original set.

5) B   Illustrates the identity axiom of addition. A illustrates additive inverse, C illustrates multiplicative inverse, and D illustrates the cornnautative axiom of addition.

6) B   In simplifying from step a to step b, 3 replaced 7 - 4, therefore the correct justification would be subtraction or substitution.

7) B   In order to be closed under division, when any two members of the set are divided the answer must be contained in the set. This is not true for integers, natural, or whole numbers as illustrated by the counter example 11/2 = 5.5.

8) D   There are an infinite number of real numbers between any two real numbers.

9) B is inappropriate. A shows a 7x4 rectangle with 3 additional units. C is the multiplication of the 28 boxes by the separate 3 boxes below. D shows how mental subtraction might be visualized leaving a composite difference.

10) A According to the order of operations, multiplication is performed first, then addition and subtraction from left to right.

11) B is always false. A,C,and D illustrate various properties of inverse relations.

12) A 12(40) = 480 which is closest to $500.

13) D 5n is always even and and even number added to an even number is always an even number, thus divisible by 2.

14) D x + y is sometimes prime. B and C show the products of two numbers which are always composite. x + y may be true, but not always, A.

15) C Choose the number of each prime factor that are in common.

16) A Although choices B, C and D are common multiples, when both numbers are even, the product can be divided by two to obtain the least common multiple.

17) B Multiply the decimals and add the exponents.

18) D Express as the fraction 1/8, then convert to a decimal.

19) C Divide the decimals and subtract the exponents.

20) D Cross multiply to obtain 12 = 8x, then divide both sides by 8.

21) C 3/8 is equivalent to .375 and 37.5%

22) C Set up the proportion 3/2 = x/5, cross multiply to obtain 15=2x, then divide both sides by 2.

23) A Let x be the wholesale price, then x + .30x = 520, 1.30x = 520. divide both sides by 1.30.

24) C There are 6 favorable outcomes: 2,4,5,6,7,8 and 8 possibilities. Reduce 6/8 to 3/4.

25) C The odds are that he will win 3 and lose 7.

26) A In this example of conditional probability, the probability of drawing a black sock on the first draw is 5/10. It is implied in the problem that there is no replacement, therefore the probability of obtaining a black sock in the second draw is 4/9. Multiply the two probabilities and reduce to loosest terms.

27) D With replacement, the probability of obtaining a butterscotch on the first draw is 2/8 and the probability of drawing a butterscotch on the second draw is also 2/8. Multiply and reduce to lowest terms.

28) A Place the numbers is ascending order: 3 6 7 11 14 20. Find the average of the middle two numbers (7+11)12 =9

29) B The median provides the best measure of central tendency in this case where the mode is the lowest number and the mean would be disproportionately skewed by the outlier $120,000.

30) C George spends $150 on food and $300 on utilities.

31) A Percentile ranking tells how the student compared to the norm or the other students taking the test. It does not correspond to the percentage answered correctly, but can indicate how the student compared to the average student tested.

32) D The greatest possible error of measurement is $\pm$ + 1/2 unit, in this case .5 cm or 5 mm.

33) C A cookie is measured in grams.

34) D To change kilometers to meters, move the decimal 3 places to the right.

35) C There are 9 square feet in a square yard.

36) B Find the radius by solving $\Pi r^2 = 25$. Then substitute r=2.82 into $C = 2\Pi r$ to obtain the circumference.

37) A Divide the figure into two rectangles with a horizontal line. The area of the top rectangle is 36 in, and the bottom is 20 in.

38) D Find the area of the square $10^2 = 100$, then subtract 1/2 the area of the circle. The area of the circle is $\Pi r^2 = (3.14)(5)(5)=78.5$. Therefore the area of the shaded region is 100 - 39.25 - 60.75.

39) C The perimeters of similar polygons are directly proportional to the lengths of their sides, therefore 9/15 = x/150. Cross multiply to obtain 1350 = 15x, then divide by 15 to obtain the perimeter of the smaller polygon.

40) B Divide the figure into a triangle, a rectangle and a trapezoid. The area of the triangle is 1/2 bh = 1/2 (4)(5) = 10. The area of the rectangle is bh = 12(10) = 120. The area of the trapezoid is 1/2(b + B)h = 1/2(6 + 10)(3) = 1/2 (16)(3) = 24. Thus, the area of the figure is 10 + 120 + 24 =154.

41) C If the radius of a right circular cylinder is doubled, the volume is multiplied by four because in he formula, the radius is squared, therefore the new volume is 2 x 2 or four times the original.

42) A Solve for the radius of the cylinder using $A = 4\Pi r^2$. The radius is 3. Then, find the volume using $4/3\ \Pi r^3$. Only when the radius is 3 are the volume and surface area equivalent.

43) B There are five surfaces which make up the prism. The bottom rectangle has area 6 x 12 = 72. The sloping sides are two rectangles each with an area of 5 x 12 = 60. The height of the prism and triangles is determined to be 4 using this Pythagorean theorem. Therefore each triangle has area 1/2bh = 1/2(6)(4) -12. Thus, the surface area is 72 + 60 + 60 + 12 + 12 = 216.

44) B Using the general formula for a pyramid V = 1/3 bh, since the base is tripled and is not squared or cubed in the formula, the volume is also tripled.

45) C The lateral area does not include the base.

46) A The reflexive property states that every number or variable is equal to itself and every segment is congruent to itself.

47) C Step 3 can be justified by the transitive property.

48) C Simplify the complex fraction by inverting the denominator and multiplying: 3/4(3/2)=9/8, then subtract exponents to obtain the correct answer.

49) A First perform multiplication and division from left to right; 7t -8t + 6t, then add and subtract from left to right.

50) B Using additive equality, $-3 \geq 4x$. Divide both sides by 4 to obtain $-3/4 \geq x$. Carefully determine which answer choice is equivalent.

51) D The quantity within the absolute value symbols must be either > 4 or < -4. Solve the two inequalities 2x + 3 > 4 or 2x + 3 < -4

52) D Multiplying the top equation by -4 and adding results in the equation 0 = -33. Since this is a false statement, the correct choice is the null set.

53) B Substituting x in the second equation results in 7(3y + 7) + 5y = 23. Solve by distributing and grouping like terms: 26y+49 = 23, 26y = -26, y = -1 Substitute y into the first equation to obtain x.

54) C By looking at the graph, we can determine the slope to be -1 and the y-intercept to be 3. Write the slope intercept form of the line as $y = -1x + 3$. Add x to both sides to obtain $x + y = 3$, the equation in standard form.

55) A Solve by adding -7 to each side of the inequality. Since the absolute value of x is less than 6, x must be between -6 and 6. The end points are not included so the circles on the graph are hollow.

56) D Be sure to enclose the sum of the number and 6 in parentheses.

57) B Let x = the speed of the boat in still water and c = the speed of the current.

	rate	time	distance
upstream	x - c	3	30
downstream	x + c	1.5	30

Solve the system:
$$3x - 3c = 30$$
$$1.5x + 1.5c = 30$$

58) B Each number in the domain can only be matched with one number in the range. A is not a function because 0 is mapped to 4 different numbers in the range. In C, 1 is mapped to two different numbers. In D, 4 is also mapped to two different numbers.

59) D Solve the denominator for 0. These values will be excluded from the domain.
$$2x^2 - 3 = 0$$
$$2x^2 = 3$$
$$x^2 = 3/2$$
$$x = \sqrt{\tfrac{3}{2}} = \sqrt{\tfrac{3}{2}} \cdot \sqrt{\tfrac{2}{2}} = \tfrac{\pm\sqrt{6}}{2}$$

60) C Glancing first at the solution choices, factor (y - x) from each term. This leaves -8 from the first term and a from the second term: $(a - 8)(y - x)$

61) D The complete factorization for a difference of cubes is $(k - m)(k^2 + mk + m2)$.

62) A Distribute and combine like terms to obtain $7x^2 - 14 = 0$. Add 14 to both sides, then divide by 7. Since $x^2 = 2$, $x = \sqrt{2}$

63) C Simplify each radical by factoring out the perfect squares:
$$5\sqrt{3} + 7\sqrt{3} - 4\sqrt{3} = 8\sqrt{3}$$

64) D The discriminate is the number under the radical sign. Since it is negative the two roots of the equation are complex.

65) B Since the vertex of the parabola is three units to the left, we choose the solution where 3 is subtracted from x, then the quantity is squared.

66) D The constant of variation for an inverse proportion is xy.

67) B $\frac{2}{6} = \frac{x}{18}$, Solve 36=6x. x=6

68) C

69) A

70) C

71) C The angles in A are exterior. In B, the angles are vertical. The angles in D are consecutive, not adjacent.

72) A Each interior angle of the hexagon measures 120°. The isosceles triangle on the left has angles which measure 120, 30, and 30. By alternate interior angle theorem, $\angle 1$ is also 30.

73) C In any triangle, an exterior angle is equal to the sum of the remote interior angles.

74) B Use SAS with the last side being the vertical line common to both triangles.

75) D Angles formed by intersecting lines are called vertical angles and are congruent.

76) B In similar polygons, the areas are proportional to the squares of the sides. 36/64 = x/64

77) A The sides are in the same ratio.

78) B The altitude from the right angle to the hypotenuse of any right triangle is the geometric mean of the two segments which are formed. Multiply 7 x 14 and take the square root.

79) A In a 30-60- 90 right triangle, the leg opposite the 30° angle is half the length of the hypotenuse.

80) D Minor arc AC measures 50°, the same as the central angle. To determine the measure of the major arc, subtract from 360.

81) B An inscribed angle is equal to one half the measure of the intercepted arc.

82) C The points marked C and D are the intersection of the circles with centers A and B.

83) C Using a compass, point K is found to be equidistant from A and B.

84) D A postulate is an accepted property of real numbers or geometric figures which cannot be proven, A, B. and C are theorems which can be proven.

85) B The point, line, and plane are the three undefined concepts on which plane geometry is based.

86) B To obtain the final side, add CD to both BC and ED.

87) D The isoscoles triangle theorem states that the base angles are congruent, and the reflexive property states that every segment is congruent to itself.

88) C Using the distance formula

$$\sqrt{[3-(-3)]^2 + (7-4)^2}$$
$$= \sqrt{36+9}$$
$$= 3\sqrt{5}$$

89) D Using the midpoint formula

$$x = (2 + 7)/2 \qquad y = (5 + -4)/2$$

90) B

91) B

92) C

93) B

94) D

95) B

96) A

97) C

98) C

99) D   100) D